And I Don't Even Like Kids

And I Don't Even Like Kids

Failing forward in Haiti

Debbie Harvey

XULON PRESS

Xulon Press
2301 Lucien Way #415
Maitland, FL 32751
407.339.4217
www.xulonpress.com

Find Debbie and Bill Harvey on the web here:
www.AngelAdvisoryGroup.com
Facebook: Facebook.com/angeladvisorygroup
Twitter: twitter.com/AngelAdvisoryGroup
Instagram: Instagram.com/AngelAdvisoryGroup
Cover Design: Photo by Hunter Kittrell Photography

Printed in the United States of America.

ISBN-13: 978-1-54563-505-6

ADVANCE PRAISE

THIS BOOK, AS WITH ALL OF DEBBIE'S LIFE, IS A REFLECTION of her heart for the Lord and for the people of Haiti. She always says that she only desires to be Christ-like, loving, and honest. This drives every heart-decision and has forever changed Haiti, as well as blessed all those who know her. The honest sharing of the lessons learned by "failing-forward" will encourage and inspire your servant's heart and strengthen your faith no matter what land He may send you to.

DEDICATION

For my husband, Bill, who dragged me kicking and screaming to Haiti.
You introduced me to a country and to a family that God gave me
a heart for.
It's because of you that our lives changed.
It's because of you that I'm blessed beyond measure. You are my best friend and my rock. You fill me up and pick me up when I'm struggling both in Haiti and at home. God brought you to me 35 years ago and I thank Him every day...for you.

ACKNOWLEDGEMENTS

I'VE WANTED TO WRITE THIS BOOK FOR YEARS. GOD had a much bigger plan. He continued to test me and our Helping Haitian Angels organization. He knew I needed more time with Him which would then bring more chapters in this book. He wanted me to learn more so that I could fail forward and pay forward information he was blessing me with so that others just beginning or struggling could benefit from all He put me (HHA) through. Did we do what we wanted to do when tested (the easy route) or do we respond by stepping out in faith while undeniably trusting Him? Do we glorify Him in each decision we make? In 2008 I made my first trip to Haiti. I had no desire to ever go to Haiti. Today our family has 59 of the most amazing, loving, funny, goofy, bright kids who all have stories of their early lives that we can't even comprehend. Many are hurting, receive psychological help and are not sure they trust or believe in God. They have all been abandoned, orphaned, unwanted. Some have had parents who tried to kill them. These are our children. The adults who work with us are just as special as the children. They are Jesus loving role models who dance, sing, help with homework, discipline and protect our children. They respect us and are grateful for their jobs. They are also our family and we adore each and every one of them. Thank you Kay Anj family for allowing me to love you.

First, I thank YOU God for choosing this crazy (ordinary, completely regular, unqualified), woman to love your Haitian children. You give me strength, courage, a team of perfectly placed people so that we do all YOU would have us do to glorify you.

We would not be able to feed or educate one child if it wasn't for our generous and supportive donors. We thank you for your belief in us and all God has us doing in Haiti. We thank you for your trust that we are using your gifts wisely and carefully. You sponsor our children which makes them the happiest children on the planet. They pray for you and wait for you to come visit. You give them hope. You let them know that they matter. Thanks to you they believe they can go on to learn at a university or become proficient at a trade. They believe they can become a doctor, teacher, seamstress, business person and a good mom and/or dad.

Thank you HHA board of directors. I've told my board and others who will listen that HHA has the best board in the whole wide world. You listen, guide, advise and you are, without question, the most supportive and faithful group of colleagues I've had the pleasure to work with. Each one of you plays a very special role at Kay Anj. God brought us all together for such a time as this.

Without Cathy Shaffer, my prayer warrior and HHA prayer team leader, I would be lost. Cathy and her team pray and fast monthly, have emergency prayer meetings (when we're in trouble in Haiti), pray for our children and volunteers by name. They have the direct line to God and we are grateful.

As for my (American) kids, they call this moms "God Job". Thank you Will, Jake and Becca, my three wonderful children. You have supported me and encouraged me to ride this crazy Haiti roller coaster since I returned from my first trip in tears 10 years ago. You have each been with dad and me in Haiti too many times to count. You love and adore your Haitian family. I know there were times I put Haiti and our family ahead of you. You knew it too. I'm sure it hurt, but you loved me and supported me through it. It was definitely difficult at times, finding the balance, but again - Will, Jake and Becca, you gave me grace and encouraged me to focus on Haiti.

Thank you Michel DeGraff (Professor Massachusetts Institute of Technology and founder of Haitian Creole Academy) and Christine Low (Matenwa Community Learning Center) for teaching me the best way to educate a child (and adults) in Haiti. Your knowledge, expertise and guidance are invaluable. Haiti is a better place thanks to you two who pioneer, champion and fight for Haiti's education system. You inspire me to provide the best for our students.

Thank you Jim Good for editing my book. You did it because you believed in what I wrote and I am grateful. Thank you Patsy for your never ending, unfailing, always faithful support for me. I adore you. Thank you Malia for agreeing to sit with me in the

Appellate courthouse on only your 2nd trip to Haiti, to give me the biggest smile and two thumbs up when during one of the scariest times in my life.

To all of our volunteers, I am humbled by the hours you spend loving our children and building relationships with them. You willingly sweat, cry, hurt and you LOVE. You get your hearts dirty, not your hands dirty. You build people and not buildings. I am grateful for your sacrifice.

TABLE OF CONTENTS

INTRODUCTION

I Don't Want to Go to Haiti

MY HUSBAND, BILL, HAD BEEN TRAVELING TO HAITI FOR five years. I had no desire to go with him. None. He stopped asking me to go after about three years and many "no thank-yous." We had three kids of our own that I was raising. One of our kids, Jake, had medical issues that demanded much time. Why would I leave my kids here in Virginia to go to Haiti for a week? No thanks. Then Bill asked one last time, but this time he asked in a way that would make it very hard for me to say "no thanks." He asked if I'd please go with him to meet his Haitian friends and family. How does a loving wife of 23 years say no to that? I told him I'd go but I wasn't going to stay the whole week as he always does, that I'd go for a few days.

The day I left for my very first trip to Haiti, on July 15, 2008, God turned my world upside down. He knew what He was doing. I didn't. Bill told me what to pack and I brought all the wrong clothes. My shorts were too short. I learned this when the Haitian kids would yell, "Cute!" "Cute!" I thought they thought I was cute! Nope, that means "short." I bought new hiking boots on Bill's suggestion. I ended up with blisters and could hardly stand the pain as I put them on each morning. I'm sure the Haitian people thought I was another American idiot coming to Haiti to "work."

On my first day in Cap Haitien we made one of the biggest mistakes you can make when serving in a developing country. We tried to make their lives "better," or what we determined to be better. Really that just meant that we tried to make their lives more like ours because ours are so much better. Right? We live in a First World country so ours must be better. Because I was coming a few days later than Bill I was the lucky one who got to drag two, huge boxes with solar ovens through the airport. I made handles out of duct tape and pulled them behind me.

I was told these ovens would help the cook mamas at an orphanage so of course I'll drag them with me. They're helping women and children in Haiti. Bill and his buddy were putting in a clean-water well in this orphanage. We couldn't wait to get to the orphanage to get the solar ovens cooking. We went into the "ville," bought a live chicken, cut its head off, cleaned him and put him in the oven with rice and beans. We, the children, and mamas watched as the oven reached 300 degrees. It's working! Everyone is laughing and dancing. We're thinking we're pretty awesome. Now these three mamas can spend their time doing all kinds of other things for the children. We freed them from their cooking duties and gave them time to do other things. Four hours later, everyone filled with anticipation, we opened the ovens. "Wow, this is really good food," everyone yelled. The kids ate everything including the bones! We celebrated. "Wahoo, look what we did!" I am so glad I dragged those darned things through the airport.

The next day when we arrived at the orphanage to finish the well we were shocked to find that our solar ovens were gone. "Where are the two solar ovens?" They cost about $300 each. "We don't know."

"Ah, what do you mean you don't know?" "Ummm, somebody took them." "Whaaat?" We later found out that our Haitian friends sold our ovens. And then it felt like I'd been punched in the stomach. What had we done? We realized later after much discussion what we had done. We didn't ask the mamas if they wanted solar ovens. We just assumed that they did. We assumed that everyone wants to free-up time and make like easier. We assumed we knew what was best for them. We assumed wrong. First, we didn't know that in Haiti women who are cooks, they only cook. They love their jobs and are proud of the food they make for the children. They take pride in the hours they sit cleaning beans, mashing veggies, cleaning chickens, and then cooking. They asked what they were supposed to do for the four hours the food was in the oven. We stole their dignity. Cooking defines these beautiful women. It's what fills them up, gives them joy. Their cooking gives them a purpose and we tried to take that from them.

We learned that the Haitian people typically don't do more than one job. If you hire a mama to do laundry when she is done doing her laundry she is not going to help the cook mamas cut up veggies for dinner. She is a laundry mama and that is where her God-given gift is. And it's what she loves to do. She is proud of her job. We learned a very important and valuable lesson that day. We call these lessons "failing-forward." We have failed-forward many, many times in Haiti. We are grateful that God has us recognize and learn from our failings so that we move forward and not make the same mistakes again.

I am writing this book so that you don't make the same mistakes we did. You will fail-forward. It's impossible not to. You will hurt people and you will get hurt by people. You will lose money. My wish for you after you read this book is that you better understand Haiti, Haitian culture, the beautiful people of Haiti, and how to work with them, not for them. I am writing this book because I believe God has taken us through trials and tests so that we learn how to love Haiti and her people using the gifts God has blessed us with. We have learned (by falling on our faces) crucial, cross-cultural lessons. We thank Him through the very tough trials and we walk in a humble obedience. We are then blessed. Blessed with information that we believe God wants us to pass on to others who have a heart for the Haitian people. You will have your heart broken if you're helping in Haiti. Our hope is that you get it broken a little less after you read this book. We want to help you navigate the legal process with your non-profit organization. We will help you understand how to purchase/lease land in Haiti. You will learn how to, and if you should, open an orphanage. We will help you understand the cultural issues when hiring and firing staff. You will learn how to bring volunteers to Haiti to learn, respect, and work with people, not do for them or take part in "voluntourism."

Chapter 1:

STARTING YOUR ORGANIZATION AND NAVIGATING THE LEGAL PROCESS IN HAITI

Psalm 91:14 : "Because he loves me," says the Lord, "I will rescue him; I will protect him, for he acknowledges my name."

HOW DO YOU START AN ORGANIZATION IN HAITI? HOW do you legalize your organization all while respecting Haitian culture, the legal system, and the people? First, you need to understand why Haiti has more non-profit organizations than any other country in the world. Why are so many people drawn to help in Haiti? Why do so many missionaries serve in Haiti? Is starting another non-profit organization in Haiti perpetuating poverty? Some say Haiti is a place where projects go to die.

There is a difference between relief and development. Relief is recognizing the need for immediate help. There is a crisis. Relief is necessary in times of natural disaster. Food, clothing, and shelter are needed when families are left with nothing after a hurricane, such as Hurricane Matthew in 2016. Development is a process. Development, if done correctly, will take time. A lot of time. Development is allowing villages and communities to positively evolve to create a lasting future for their local families, schools, churches, and ultimately generations to come. Development is finding local leaders, empowering them to be leaders for their communities. Allowing them to make decisions that will have a positive effect on their local families. Everyone must understand the role they've been given. We also have our role. I wonder if most of us understand ours. Haiti may be the most difficult country in the world to see true transformation. Haiti is a true contradiction. It is filthy, corrupt, deforested, and dark, but also faithful, beautiful, fruitful, and appreciative. We do not want the Haitian people to think that we are the hero. The knight riding in on the white horse saving the day. We cannot save the day for them. We cannot be the hero and we should not be either of these for them. When we are we provide our Haitian friends with an unhealthy dependency. We are not the leaders. We are guests in their county. We should never do for anyone, even children, what they can do for themselves.

After finding the 35 or so children on that day in 2008, Bill and decided after my prayer-and-wises council that we would find a place for the children to live. A place with a roof, beds, mattresses, sheets, clean water, and food. We didn't know at the time that we were opening an orphanage. How do we make this legal? Can we get grant money? We didn't have any extra income and had three children of our own that would soon need college tuition. We had a party/fundraiser at our house and told people not to show up unless they brought their checkbook. They came and wanted to hear more. Most wrote checks that night. We raised $16,000 that would be our seed money to start Helping Haitian Angels (HHA).

HHA is a Christian organization that seeks to provide a future for our orphaned and abandoned children and our Haitian staff. We built family homes that house up to 10 children and a mama or mama and papa. We built a school that provides a cutting-edge, mother-tongue education to our children and 100-plus children from the local communities. We built a non-denominational, open-to-anyone-and-everyone Baptist church. We also provide a training and life-skills program for our "transitional" young adults.

Why did we start an orphanage? Honestly, I don't really like children. My children didn't have many playgroups, as I didn't like other kids coming to my house asking for food, using my bathroom, and tearing up my house. Just not my thing. Why would God ask me to rescue abandoned children? Why me? I had no idea but I knew He had a plan.

Were Bill and I scared? Absolutely. Because we respect Haiti and the laws of the country we knew we needed to be completely legal. This takes time in a country like Haiti. We met with an attorney friend in the U.S. to begin the process of legalizing our non-profit organization. We applied for our 501c3 non-profit status in the U.S. We then met with a Haitian friend in Cap Haitien, Haiti who guided us on the steps to become legal in Haiti, also. Bill and I applied for and got the equivalent of a Haitian Social Security number. We formed a Haitian Board of Directors that had to have nine people of both Haitians and Americans. We had to register with the local mayor and DGI (Department of Land Records, Tax, etc.).

We had to apply for a Quitus, which any operating business in Haiti must have and display.

We also had to legalize our orphanage with the IBESR, the equivalent of Children's Social Services. Finding an honest, trustworthy attorney is no easy feat in Haiti. All of these processes take months and months and a lot of money. You will be told on Friday to go to this office to apply for a legal document. You go on Friday, the person you need to speak to is not in yet (and it's noon), no one else can help you so you sit and wait. And wait. The person finally shows up and tells you that you need another document before you can come to him. Where do I need to go for that document, sir? It's downstairs in this building, madam. You could've gone and applied for the first document while you waited for him to show up and now it's Friday at 3 p.m. and that office is closed for the weekend. We begin again on Monday. Many do not legalize their organizations because of the attorney's fees and cost to complete documents alone.

I cannot strongly enough recommend that you build relationships with both Haitians and foreigners (Americans, Europeans, Asian) in Haiti. We are all there to serve, love, and learn from the Haitian people. You will only do that more authentically and more personally if you have people you trust that you can go to when you have questions, you need advice, or you want to vent. Don't reinvent the wheel that someone else has already invented, especially when that wheel is turning well. Ask people who they use for an attorney. Do they trust him/her? Are their fees reasonable? Do they communicate well? Interview at least three attorneys and then pray.

Your new attorney will tell you that you need him to apply for your Permis De Sejour. I wish someone had told me to apply as soon as I knew I'd be working in Haiti for the long haul. Here's why. In 2010, just after the devastating earthquake in Port au Prince that killed approximately 300,000 people, we brought on a Haitian, Baptist pastor to manage our orphanage when we were not in the country. I remember Bill saying to me, "Let's hire him, if a man of God steals from us then we're leaving Haiti." Well, that so-called man of God did much more than steal from us. He tried to take our land, and all we gave to our children. He was loving and prayerful when we first met him. It appeared that the children embraced their new Papa, too. When we found the land that our homes are built on today we needed to put our trustworthy pastor's name on all legal documents, as we were not Haitian and did not have our Permis De Sejour at that time. We trusted Pastor Pierre. He was family. He brought in very sick children who had no parents. At least that's what we were told.

After a couple of years of the kids toys going missing, clothes and books missing, and pillows and sheets missing, we started to wonder about the trustworthiness of our wonderful Pastor Pierre. Red flags began to appear. We questioned the amount of tuition we were paying for a local public school. We would enroll all 39 of our children. We were told the total for each child was $190 for the year. This included tuition, uniforms, books, and a snack. We raised the money and paid for all of our kids to go to school. We then asked a friend to take his two young daughters to the school to inquire about registration/tuition. He was told it would be $80 for the year including uniforms and books.

We were devastated when we learned that our beloved pastor had charged us more than double for each child to go to school. We later learned that he and the school director shared the extra money we'd paid. That was it. We knew it was time for him to leave our orphanage and our organization. He was beyond angry when we asked for his resignation. It took him a week to agree to give it to us. In Haiti there is a formula that is paid to the employee even if they have been fired or resign for cause. We sat at the Notary's office with our first attorney in Haiti. The office was so small it only fit a desk and two chairs. The desk left just enough room for the attorney to squeeze into his chair. I didn't mind it as it was air-conditioned. We sat in this cramped office as we asked our pastor to remover his name from all of our legal documents. We realized quickly that on paper our pastor technically owned the land we'd worked two years to legally acquire. He knew this, too. As we sat so close that we were almost in each other's lap, he looked me strait in my face and said he'd remove his name for $80,000 U.S. dollars. I was dumbfounded.

What did you just say, Pas? Did you say $80,000? U.S.? You know we don't have that kind of money. I put my head in my hands and tried to cry but I was so angry the tears just wouldn't come. I didn't look up as I was still trying to make myself cry when Pas said, "Is it the money you're upset about?" *What do you think, Pas?! Of course it's the money. We don't have it and we treated you like family. How could you do this to us?* Then it hit me. I needed to pray and pray intentionally. I asked for a few minutes to get myself together. I prayed. I prayed for wisdom, the perfect words, and guidance. I walked back in and squeezed into my little chair. I told Pas that God told me it would all be OK. That we didn't need him to remove himself from the documents. He looked confused and stunned. I think he just realized he wasn't going to hit the lottery today.

I told him that there was plenty of land in Haiti for us to build on and when God closes a door, He opens a window. I stood up as if to end the meeting. Pas said, "Tann, tann (wait, wait)." He said, "I'll take $30,000 dollars." I looked at him confidently and peacefully and said, "Pas, God will bring us the land He wants us to build our village on. Clearly this is not where He wants us to be." I really did not want to do this as we had worked tirelessly for two years to acquire this beautiful, loved property. Again I stood up to end the meeting, went to shake his hand and thank him for the few years working with us. Again he said, "Tann, tann." I told him that we'd give him a small bonus for all the work he'd done for us in return for him removing his name from all of our documents. Seething mad, Pas agreed. He was so mad that when the attorney had the documents ready to sign he couldn't be in the same room with me. The attorney said he was acting like a "monst," which means monster in Haitian Kreyol. I was on my knees that night in my hotel room thanking God for His words and His direction. There are times, especially in Haiti, that we stand back and say, "There is no other answer, but God." Unfortunately, Pas didn't leave quietly. When friends from his church heard about all that had happened, and that he didn't get the pay-off he thought he was going to get, they too were very angry. They marched up the hill to our orphanage and threw rocks and bottles over the walls into the main area where our kids play and study. Kids were screaming and hiding. I got a call and was told to get to the orphanage immediately. I asked the night guard who was working at our hotel if he'd go with me as he was in uniform and was carrying a rifle. He agreed to go with me if I paid him.

We arrived at our front gate 15-minutes later to find crying, hysterical children and mama's. Our night guard, Jean, would not let us in. We called the police who were able to get us in. Most people are very afraid of the police in Haiti. Two of our oldest girls were crying so hard they could hardly breath. Our guard had kicked one of the girls in the chest because of something that happened to her years before. Rosa had been raped by her father at the tender age of 13. She gave birth to her father's baby when she was just 14. Her mother kicked her out of the home, and sweet Rosa was there on that fateful day on my first trip. We buried the story because we knew it would only bring severe pain to Rosa and her baby. Our guard, Jean, learned of the story and used it against us to hurt one of our children because we didn't give Pas what he wanted.

We decided to fire Jean that evening. We sat with him and told him because he kicked one of our children he would no longer have a job with us. We told him we would file proper documents with the Department of Labor the next day. Jean wouldn't leave so our armed security guard and the police escorted him out of our orphanage, as he carried his little box of possessions that he kept in the guard room. Minutes later I got a call that I must go right now to the police station. *Hadn't we been through enough tonight?*

I reluctantly got in the truck and headed to see what the police wanted. There were seven chairs in a perfect circle with one chair in the middle. They first asked me to sit in the middle seat as the police chief and police officers sat in the circle around me. They asked me to tell my side of the story. It didn't take long but I stated the facts. Then they asked Jean to sit in the middle chair and do the same. When they heard him say that he asked for $75,000 they laughed and said, "Even President Martelly couldn't get $75,000 if he left his job." They told Jean to give me the keys to front gate. He said no. They quickly reminded him that if anything happened to any of the kids while he had the keys, he would be responsible. He threw the keys across the circle of chairs at me.

The next morning we met with the same attorney in the same tiny office. Jean got nothing more than the Department of Labor's required amount. That was it. It was finally over. If you plan on staying in Haiti longer than three months, you will need to apply for your Permis De Sejour. You also need it if you plan on putting your name on legal documents. It's a bit of a pain to put all of your documents together, but it's well worth it. The law states that every person over the age of 21 who travels with a non-Haitian, travel document (U.S. Passport), and who intends to remain in Haiti for more than three months, for whatever reason, is required to obtain a Permis de Sejour. This includes missionaries, teachers, businessmen, retirees, and students. Applications for this document can be made in Haiti at the Direction de l'Immigration in Port au Prince.

Again, it's a long, tedious, and frustrating process. I don't have enough fingers to count the number of times I went back to the Immigration office to pick up my Permis only to learn it wasn't there...again. Having your Permis allows you to live in Haiti for five years. An even bigger advantage is that it allows you to put your own name (and not a Haitian working with you) on legal documents. And for that alone it was well worth the time, money, and frustration. I have a list of all required documents and process that I can provide for you.

Chapter 2:

SHOULD WE OPEN AN ORPHANAGE?

"I won't leave you like orphans. I will come back to you." -John 14:8

IT ALL BEGAN IN JULY OF 2003. MY HUSBAND, BILL, went on his first trip to Haiti with a good friend from church. For five years Bill gently asked me to go with him. I continually (not so gently) said, "no thank-you." I had three children of my own, one with medical issues, and I had zero desire to travel to Haiti. In July of 2008 Bill said this, "I'd love you to go with me to meet my Haitian friends and family." Now I had to go. He'd asked differently this time and I knew God wanted me to go with him to meet all the wonderful people he'd spend time with over the past five years.

On day two of my short, four-day trip (I'd told him I'd go but not for an entire week like he does!), a neatly-dressed woman tugged at my arm. In a language I didn't understand she was asking me to come with her to see some very sick children. My husband told her we had other work to do and couldn't go. I was shocked. He loves kids and is in Haiti to help. How could he tell her no? The next day the same woman found us in a small market where we were buying PVC pipe to finish a clean-water well at an orphanage. She begged me again to come with her to see the kids. My husband, at my insistence, told her we had 10 minutes and that's all. We had no idea what we were about to find. There were five of us, me, Bill, a friend and his father, and a Methodist minister.

When we walked into the falling-down, lean-to that the kids were "living" in we stood in shock. It was as if our feet were in cement. We couldn't move. *What do we do? How do we help? How did this happen?* There were 35 or so kids, with no adults, and all sick. Most could hardly hold their heads up. They had open, golf-ball-size wounds on their thighs. Most had a bad case of worms and orange-tinted hair from lack of protein and iron. The kids could hardly hold their heads up but the lady had them sing a song to us. The pastor and I had to quietly walk out to process what we were seeing and to breathe. *What had we just seen?* It was horrific. Children should not have to live this way. My pastor friend vomited.

We pulled ourselves together and went back in to assess the situation with the kids. *What do we do? How do we help? Who do we know? How much will it cost?* We started with an American pediatrician, a friend we knew from Bill's trips to Haiti. Dr. Ray Ford checked in on the kids and told us that half will most likely die before our next trip back in six months (yes, Bill talked me into returning). He gave us a bag of Albendazol, a deworming pill, for each child. We bought a box of mismatched clothes and a box of towels from the market. We also gave them clean water and powdered milk. Then we left. James 1:27 says to care for the orphans. We provided all we could that day and we left for home.

I couldn't sleep. I cried and cried for the sick and dying children I'd met. *God why did you have us meet them? Why aren't you helping them?* I woke Bill up at 3 a.m. two nights after returning home. I told him that we had to help these children. He told me to "give it

30 days and if you still want to do something we'll talk then." Three nights later, again at 3 a.m., I woke him and told him I can't and won't give it 30 days. We need to help and we need to help now. Bill listened and knew that I'd made my mind up and we were going to do something. But what? We knew nothing about starting an orphanage and as far as I know there's no manual to help those who want to open an orphanage. But if I knew then what I know today we most likely wouldn't have opened an orphanage on that day in 2008.

You see, many of the children we found and rescued had a parent or caregiver. This is true of almost all orphanages in developing countries. Parents simply cannot care for their children so they, through many different routes, get them in an orphanage. The parent hopes and prays the child will then go to school, have nutritious food, clean water, and clothes. The parents are OK with giving their children over to an orphanage because they believe they will be well taken care of and be given the gift of an education. They know that their children would not have the opportunity to go to school If they grew up in their home. Public school in Haiti is not free and is mediocre at best. It is common for teachers not to show up for days or even weeks in a row because they have not been paid. In the minds of the parents, life in an orphanage is much better for their children than the life they can provide for them. In an orphanage they have a shot at a better future. They have hope and they can dream of finishing their education and one day helping their parents and families. So, the parent or guardian of the child finds a group of children and puts their child/children with the group and leaves. They hope and pray a nice group of "blans" (foreigners) will find the children and want to take care of them. That's exactly what we did.

It was a textbook scam. We were taken. We took the bait hook, line, and sinker. The woman that tugged at me on my first trip was able to reach my heart. She succeeded at her plan. Please understand that I don't regret for a second that we now have 58 wonderful children in our care. And orphanages are necessary for children that are true orphans. I only wish I would have known then what I know today. I would have done things differently, for sure. We prayed and cried a lot in the early years. Bill and I almost divorced a few times. I became a bit obsessed with helping and providing for the kids. I reminded Bill that it was all his fault as he was the one who dragged me to Haiti that first trip (kicking and screaming).

Now let's understand why opening an orphanage is not the best thing to do for the children you want to help. First, the majority of children have at least one parent. Most of the families want their children and truly want to care for them, but with no support from their community or government the parents feel they have no choice other than to place their children into an orphanage. Years and years of documented research teaches us that children raised in institutional orphanages fare much worse than children raised with their families, even if their family does not have the means to provide an education.

Now, let's move on to reunification. Family reunification is the process of returning and reuniting an orphaned and/or abandoned child in temporary or permanent out-of-home care, back to the family of the child. As we said earlier, all of the research suggests that children have a more successful future when raised with the biological families as opposed to institutional-orphanage living. When we first opened our orphanage over nine years ago we were told by the trusted pastor managing all for us that the children had no parents and could not survive if we didn't help them. We later learned that most of the children had family and most were given to the pastor to take care of. He may have been paid by the parents. After many trials and tests by God we learned more and more about the problem of reunification, orphanages, and orphan care. We decided to do our due diligence and reunify our children with their families. It's what's best for them. Or is it?

In 2014, we were approached by a grassroots, non-profit organization in Cap Haitien that had been chosen to participate in a documentary highlighting them as an organization making changes for the women and children of Northern Haiti. The organization's mission is to provide jobs to moms in Haiti so they can earn a sustainable living wage, provide for their children, and keep their families together. Ultimately there would be less children in orphanages and more families living together. The organization needed a mother and daughter to film for the documentary. They contacted us and yes, we were in the process of reuniting our precious seven-year-old, Angeline, with her loving mother, Rezilia. Rezilia has seven children and placed Angeline in our orphanage years earlier, as she could not provide for her.

The organization provided Rezilia with a job, and a couple of months later mother, daughter, and siblings were all reunified. Three years later Rezilia still works at this organization and is able to provide a stable, protective, and loving home life for all of her children. While I believe reunification is the best option in most cases I don't believe it is best for all families.

Phodline and her two brothers were brought to our village in February of 2016. They were starving and very sick. Because we're now less naïve to people telling us both parents are dead, I told the neighbor who brought them that I'd like to go see where they live. "Right now?" she asked. "Yes, right now. Let's go." We climbed a mountain that was straight uphill and if you lost your footing or diverted your attention for a second you'd roll all the way down hitting many trees on the way. We finally made it to the very small (4 feet by 4 feet) hut, made of sticks and mud that they slept in. There were no parents to be found. We were told that mom had died and dad was living in the Dominican Republic and had no plans of returning.

The three children were left to fend for themselves. They were seven, five and three.

What we saw and experienced was unimaginable for these children. We spoke with the woman who brought them to our village and told her that we would contact the IBESR and then bring them to live with us at Kay Anj. We later walked with them down the mountain and put them in our car to head to their new home. They vomited in the car as they'd never been in a car or off the mountain, for that matter. Five months later their mother came to visit them at our village. Their mother? She passed away. At least that's what we'd been told. I left the parent meeting I was in and ran to our church to meet mom.

Mom, Dani Jean, was in tears and said she too was in the Dominican Republic trying to find a job to care for her three children. We brought Phodline, Phodless, and Smith to be with their mom for a while. We carefully and thoughtfully watched their behavior. Did they appear to love their mom? Was she affectionate towards them? Did it look like mom loved her children? We sat with them for a couple of hours and then we all prayed. All of our mama's, Naomi (our American intern), and I sat on the porch and prayed.

We prayed for guidance, wisdom, and a clear path. We all felt it was best to reunify Phodless, Phodline, and Smith with their mother. We knew this would be very hard but we believed it was right for mom and her children. We gathered their pillows, clothes, backpacks, said goodbye to their new family, and drove them all back up the mountain. Dani Jean did not ask us to keep the kids but she also was not happy to be going home with her kids. We told her we'd come the next day to pay for the first semester of school tuition. We only pay a semester at a time so that if the kids don't go we are not out of an entire year's school tuition. We also told her that we will check on them weekly and bring rice and beans. We tried to get her a job at the same organization where we helped Rezilia get a job, but mom missed the interview.

Five weeks later, Dani Jean and Phodline (5-year-old girl) are found standing at our front gate asking for our head mama, Adeline. Precious little Phodline had 2nd and 3rd degree burns on her face, shoulders, and armpits. She had a couple other smaller burns on her buttocks. Adeline quickly put them in our truck, grabbed Harry, our driver, and drove to meet me. A doctor friend staying at the same hotel as us examined Phodline. He put burn cream on her and wrapped her up. We asked mom how the burns happened. She told us that Phodline's 5-year-old cousin touched her with a burning, plastic, juice bottle. We knew this wasn't possible. Phodline later told us that someone used a piece of a burning tire to burn her. We sat and spoke lovingly and honestly with Dani Jean while others took care of Phodline.

"Did you burn Phodline, Dani Jean?" "No, I could never do that." "Do you love Phodline and her brothers, Dani Jean?" She sat there for what seemed like an hour. She then said something that I'll never forget. Dani Jean told me that she cannot love her children because she cannot take care of them. I felt like I'd been punched in the gut. I couldn't breathe. *How could a mother not love her children? And how could a mother honestly say that she cannot love her children?* At that moment Adeline and I made the decision to bring the kids back to our Kay Anj Village. We asked Dani Jean if she wanted the kids to come back with us and she said yes. We gave her a few dollars for a tap tap (taxi) and told her to get the boys ready that we'd be by in a couple of hours to pick them up. We did not say anything about returning to Kay Anj to Phodline.

When our truck arrived as high as it could drive up the mountain we saw Dani Jean and her two little boys standing there. The boys quickly jumped in our truck. Phodless grabbed Phodline's hands and said, "Phodline, we're going back to the orphanage! We're going back to live with the kids!" Phodline began to jump and scream with her brother. We'd never seen two happier kids. Smith was happy to sit with a lollipop and watch his brother and sister dance and scream with excitement.

When we arrived back at Kay Anj, our kids and mama's had a welcome-home party for the "Phodes," as we affectionately call the three. They felt loved here. They felt protected and safe. They are now home. The doctor checked on Phodline regularly. She healed well. At least the burns did. We have a child psychologist who comes regularly to meet with our kids. They say Phodline and her brothers are healing. Did we do the right thing by attempting to reunify the Phodes and their mother? I had a very hard time with this. I prayed and believed we were doing the right thing for Dani Jean and her children. But was reunifying them the best for them? I felt responsible for Phodline's burns. If I had not reunited the family she wouldn't have been burned. This was another fail-forward in Haiti for me. In the end I believe I'd make the same decision all over again. We know reunification most of the time is best for the child. I learned because of Phodline and Dani Jean that sometimes it's not. Sometimes the mother, out of sheer undeniable desperation, will harm her child to get them back into a loving, nurturing orphanage.

I believe Dani Jean loves her children. This is hard to understand but I believe that she loved them so much that she harmed them so that they'd have a chance at a future. I also believe that if Dani Jean was able to care for her children they would be with her today.

The UN Convention on the Rights of the Child (CRC) says that "for the full and harmonious development of his or her personality" the children should "grow-up in a family environment, in an atmosphere of happiness, love, and understanding." I'm not saying don't open an orphanage. I'm just saying to do it right and thoughtfully and respectfully. Make sure you're doing it in the best interest of the child. Don't do it because you want to take care of kids and you want to feel good because you've opened an orphanage to save children. I was conflicted about this for a long time. *Did we do the right thing? Should our children be living with their families. What's best for them?* We did our due diligence and spent hours upon hours researching, talking to others who'd gone before us and learned that the best way to raise an orphaned and/or abandoned child is NOT institutional-style living.

Bill and I vowed to the Lord and to each other to always treat the Haitian children in our care the same way we treat our American children. They are all God's gifts. After much studying and learning we determined that building family homes would be best for the children. We built eight homes that would house up to 10 children, and also a mama, or mama and papa. Each home has two bathrooms, room for 10 beds (not bunk beds), a private bedroom for the house parent, and a large front porch for family mealtime and outdoor living. We built a primary school in our small village that provides a cutting-edge education for preschoolers through 6th grade.

Our Kay Anj church is open to all who want to come in to praise and worship. The first priority of our house parent's is to love each of the children in their care. Corporal punishment is the primary method to get children to obey, listen, and behave in Haiti. We, at HHA, do not subscribe to this method. We help them to understand that parenting our children is their God gift. Parenting is an altar where they encounter God. We ask them what kind of father God is to them? Is he full or wrath and anger? Does he punish you for your sins? Or is He a peaceful, loving God that forgives by grace? We teach our parents to understand and give the gift of a clear path toward understanding God's unconditional love toward their children. If we believe that God is filled with wrath, judgment, disappointment, and anger, then of course that comes out in who we are and how we behave toward our children.

Parenting is for most of us where we are able to deal with our selfishness, our pride, our pet sins, our bad habits, our carefully-hidden real selves. And by contrast if we know that God is filled with love and patience, kindness and gentleness, joy and peace, faithfulness, goodness, and self-control, then that changes us and it changes how we move through our lives. We often parent our children the way that we believe God parents us. We ask our Kay Anj house parents, how do you believe God is parenting you? I am a grown woman with a family of my own and yet I am still thriving because of the security and rest, strength, and safety of my parents' love towards me. I pray that I can give that same gift to my own children. American and Haitian children alike. And he's the father who watches the road for that ungrateful and rebellious child long past hope. He is the Father who throws his arms around a child who is a bit tough to love. Our foundation is built on love. If we and our house parents have love and truly love our children, they believe in themselves and know that there are people who think I'm a pretty cool kid. They trust and have faith that with God at the helm they can finish school, go on to university or professional school, provide for a family, and change their beautiful country.

Chapter 3:

MISSION TRIPS, NOT "VOLUNTOURISM"

Philippians 2:3: "In humility, consider others as more important than yourselves."

I AM SITTING IN MY RUSTIC BUT COMFORTABLE LITTLE house at our village in Limonade, Haiti this week getting ready to receive the second of two mission-trip groups this month. I look forward to the volunteers coming and I also can't wait until the trips are finished. We are the sending organization. We are responsible for the actions of our volunteers. When they are in Haiti they are the face of Helping Haitian Angels. This is a responsibility that we don't take lightly. We need to educate our volunteers prior to their first foot hitting Haitian soil. We teach cross-cultural servanthood and respect for Haiti and her people. It's on us and it is on you, too, if you bring volunteers with you to Haiti or any other developing country.

Our children are not zoo animals. They have been abandoned one too many times. They all have attachment disorders and it is imperative that you do not continue this cycle for these precious children. Again, we have failed-forward here. When we didn't know any better we brought in beanie babies, toys, balls, coloring books and crayons, crafts and candy. These children have nothing so why wouldn't we want to shower them with gifts and candy? Let me explain why we shouldn't do these things. We are not heroes; we are not saviors. We do not want the children and people of Haiti to think we are anything close to a hero or savior. With too much incoming gifts, we overwhelm the kids and adults. Giving them a coloring book with 50-pages of animals and a box of 16 crayons is simply too much. They are much happier with much less. Take one coloring book, tear out a page for each child and hand them one crayon (they can trade with other children for different colors) and they will sit quietly and happily color for an hour. Another problem you have when you bring in too much is that the staff at the orphanage or hospital will take the gifts from the children and sell them. The kids end up with nothing because you gave too much.

Now, let's talk about bringing in supplies for the kids. What are supplies? Clothes? Hygiene products? Hair-care items? Shoes? I've even heard of groups collecting canned goods. Guess what? All of these items can be purchased in Haiti. Here's how it works: You or your church group ask friends, family, and everyone you know on Facebook, to collect these items for the kids in Haiti that you're going to visit next month. Your friends feel good that they can help in some small way. They go to Wal-Mart and buy all of the items on your list of supplies for our trip to Haiti. You then pack them in your 50-pound bags, put brightly-colored duct tape on each (so that you know they belong to your group), you pay a custom's fee because your group of 20, with brand-new, bright-green T-shirts (that have something to do with saving Haiti on them) all stand together at the airport practically screaming, "We're one big group with tons and tons of supplies so you need to charge us," and you pay the custom's men who look through your bags and you are off to give away all the supplies you collected.

Here's what you did. You spent time collecting supplies for a country that needs us to purchase all that THEY sell to help THEIR economy. You put Haitian adults out of business, or at the very least, kept them from feeding their families for that week. Almost all of the items you collected can be found in the markets in Haiti. When you bring in supplies and give them away for free you are preventing people from purchasing the same items from the entrepreneurs on the streets and in the marketplaces. When they don't sell their wares, their children don't eat. YOU are responsible, as the sending organization, that you inform your volunteers so they don't do "drives" or collections. You have been called to Haiti so treat her right.

Now, let's get back to why we shouldn't wear fluorescent-colored T-shirts as we arrive in Haiti. To put it simply, you are screaming, "We have come to save the day!" You cannot save the day for them on a one-week mission trip. It's not possible. We've talked about supplies, now let's talk about projects. We know projects are necessary, but let's do them right. If you truly love the country of Haiti, her people, and especially the children, you will want to do projects in a way that builds a healthy community for your Haitian friends. I know lots of mission teams that after traveling talk about all of the relationships that they formed and how precious they were, but they were never the reason for traveling in the first place. They always come secondary to projects that detract from our human need for hearts and spirits that are willing to dance with our own.

I know how counterintuitive it seems, but why don't we forget all about our good-intended projects and programs and make our only mission be other people? Why don't we make our volunteer trips nothing more than vehicles for people's stories to travel and grow and reach their full potential? Why don't we make that the goal and just see what happens? In our organization we teach our volunteers that they will get their hearts dirty, not their hands dirty, and they will build PEOPLE, not buildings. In the end we must PARTNER WITH and empower those we've come to serve. I have brought hundreds and hundreds of mission trip volunteers to Haiti and have learned that all have a heart to serve. All want to help the people of Haiti. All mean well. But, their good intentions and compassion do not always serve the people of Haiti well and can even cause harm. Research has proven that most mission trips encourage dependency, hurt those being served, and foster dishonest relationships. When we do for those in need we steal their dignity and disempower them. We must do WITH them and not FOR them.

Should we give money to the man or group of young boys begging as soon as we step out of the airport? If you think yes, you'd be better off to just slap them in the face. It would hurt less. When you give in to their begging you are perpetuating the cycle of poverty and reinforcing their belief that we foreigners, "blans," can save them. A better answer would be to spend a minute with them and ask them what gifts God has given them? How can you help me at my village, clinic, school, or construction site? Hire them for a day and pay them for their good work. You will have empowered them to believe they are capable of more than begging. Let's build up producers, not beggars. Do most of these short-term mission trips bring lasting change? I don't think so, unless they're done differently. Again, you do not need to reinvent the wheel. Reach out to organizations who are putting their volunteers through a cultural-learning process before they head out to meet the beautiful people they will spend time with. We need to believe that our ideas of what is the best way to help may need to be transformed. I believe the two best ways to empower people to become dependency-free is to build relationships, and then give jobs. Build relationships first in the community you are spending your time in. Listen, really listen to their plans and dreams. Allowing them to be heard shows them that you respect them. And then work WITH them.

In March of this year our neighbors tore down and then burned our large, wooden, orphanage sign. It was on the main road and told people how to get to our Kay Anj Village. They then burned tires, and came yelling, screaming and wielding machetes so that we could not leave our village. This is not the first time they've done this. Threats and fear are how these men have been raised to communicate. We had a group of Ohio State University young women here and they were scared. We asked the police to do a "drive-by." They don't like the police. We had worked for years to develop a relationship with them. We wanted to always be respectful, good neighbors. We put a clean-water well in their community so that they didn't have to walk the mile to get water to cook with. Their children come into our village to go to our school where they're receiving a cutting-edge education. We provide tarps during flooding, and they are invited (some attend) to our church each weekend. When we have doctors and dentists come to our village we invite them in. They are grateful.

But, why did they burn our sign and threaten us? We invited our neighbors to a meeting and 40 showed up. We listened for over an hour as they pointed fingers, raised their voices, stomped in anger, and in the end we learned that they wanted jobs. Here is the tough part. We have 17 from our local community on our payroll as we understand and know the importance of giving jobs to our local community, our neighbors. We couldn't fault them for wanting to work and provide food for their families, but we reiterated that we have 17 of your family members on our payroll. We just don't have 40 more jobs for all of you. They didn't like that answer. So, as we do in all of our time in Haiti, we prayed. We prayed a lot. We believe God blessed us with a powerful and fair plan.

We would ask the 40 people who their community leaders are. They should pick three leaders and we would meet with this group weekly to discuss community concerns, issues, and job openings. They liked this idea and chose their "council." We later met with the council and again we listened. They wanted people in our community to have jobs. We worked together to come up with a plan that would hopefully bring peace again to our community. We would hire five men on the first of the month and another five men on the 15th of the month to cut grass for us. This is not easy work as they use machetes and spend hours in the hot sun. Each group of men would work for five days and be paid on the fifth day. The council chose the men they wanted to work. We learned that it's much more effective to allow our community to come up with their own solutions. This is painfully slow but is the only way to a successful relationship. We must not fix things for them. They need to be in control; we do not if we want to see progress in our communities. We continue this program today. It is a process. A slow and thoughtful process to truly and authentically be good neighbors to our Haitian friends and family.

Mission trips need to be less drive-in, drive-by, and more spend time with and love. Just this week I was leaving Haiti with our July mission group. There were six of us traveling home together. We were to leave Cap Haitien airport at 5:40 p.m. The flight was completely full. As we began picking up speed down the runway we made an abrupt stop. The pilot came on the loud speaker and said that our "check engine light" came on. After two hours working on the light the pilot then informed us that he would be over his legal time to fly if we didn't leave within 41 minutes. Forty-five-minutes later we were told that the flight would leave at 9 a.m. the next morning. Our flight had been cancelled for the night. I had a feeling this might happen so I contacted a friend who owns a hotel and reserved her last two rooms. I called another friend who works at the airport to ask him to get us a taxi van to take us to the hotel in the event that American Airlines cancels our flight. They did. We deplaned with almost 200 other people. The airport was closed and no one would be allowed to sleep inside. There were a few groups (in their brightly-colored T-shirts) who were panicked. They didn't know where to go, who to call, or where they'd sleep. There are only a few hotels in Cap Haitien and all were booked.

We noticed two young women who looked like they were about to cry. "Do you have a place to go," I asked. "Well, a man told us he'd get us a room but we don't know him." I told them to come with us and we'd all share our two rooms. We then ran into two sisters who also had nowhere to go. They came with us, too. We arrived safely at our hotel, were able to get a bite to eat, and slept comfortably until rising at 4 a.m. to meet our driver to get us back to the airport by 5 a.m.

Later that day we saw a link to CBS Chicago News that highlighted a "church group held in limbo in Haiti." It was terrible. They talked about being fearful of going to jail because immigration had left for the evening. They couldn't get any help from the U.S. Embassy or American Airlines. One of our trip volunteers replied to the CBS link and said it perfectly, "It comes down to Love vs. Fear. I was with an organization that is called to Haiti to love and build relationships. The other group was lost in fear of the people they claimed they came to help. HHA builds people, not buildings, and in our time of need the people of Haiti showed-up to love and help us."

Relationships win every time. I believe we need to move away from feeling good because we're doing projects and programs and focus more sincerely on people we are spending our time with. Build relationships and people, not buildings. I believe we need to walk humbly with the people of Haiti. We need to be Christ-like, and loving and honest (our organization's mantra) in every step we take. Mission trips begin with a problem because most of the needs of the people who will be served are decided upon by the church or team and seldom do we ask those on the receiving end. The real issue when we define people based on what they need is that we truly miss out on getting to know who they really are. How do we "do" mission trips as the sending organization with cross-cultural respect at the forefront? Our organizations need to exist only for the purpose of building relationships with people that live in different cultures and have different needs. Become ambassadors for the people you're spending the week with. Teams should be kept small to facilitate the greatest possible relationship-building.

We require our groups to take a six-part, Serve Smart course that is graded. We require them to read two books we believe teach cross-cultural respect. We spend time learning very basic phrases in Haitian Kreyol. We meet in person or online if out of the area twice before departure day. Our now wiser and educated volunteers come to live with and do life with our Kay Anj family and our Decle community families. Our volunteers learn about their culture and their lives. They will spend all of their time investing in their personal relationship with their new friends. We spend each morning in devotional time where we use biblical scripture and team-building to teach them about Haitian culture and language. We want our volunteers to become ambassadors for Haiti. After spending their time getting to know each other, both sides can decide to what extent they want to pursue the relationship further. Just like real people do.

Our team then goes home. They go home and talk to friends, family, church members, and work colleagues about all they learned in Haiti. They tell them that what we see in the media here in the U.S. is not always correct or fair. We expect that our trip volunteers return to continue their new relationships on future trips. Almost all do. There would be no unsuccessful projects due to lack of cultural understanding. The volunteers will not promise to come back and give them money to build a school or business hoping to do some sort of good. We are simply people investing in relationships with other people. We are not trying to help someone, but we are each given the opportunity to spend time with a family whose story we want to become a part of. We both then decide if we'd like to take the chance to take the relationship further. We must find the God-given gifts and talents the people of Haiti have been given. No matter how destitute they are they are intelligent, resourceful, and faithful people.

Chapter 4:

DEALING WITH THE CORRUPTION AND HOW TO HELP

"Finally, be strong in the Lord and in his mighty power. Put on the full armor of God, so that you can take your stand against the devil's schemes. -Ephesians 6:10-11

I DIDN'T KNOW ABOUT THE CORRUPTION IN HAITI WHEN I first started going regularly in 2008.

Everyone was nice to me, smiled at me, wanted my help. A lot of these people from my early year set me up. Today I'm jaded and this saddens me. I have been lied to, stolen from, threatened, and had voodoo thrown on me. Haiti is hard. Please know that I'm not speaking of all Haitians. Many are honest and trustworthy. Many are not. On December 14, 2014, our 47 kids, nine mama's, and our teachers were evicted at gunpoint from their homes. Eighteen UDMO (military) police showed up with AR-15's and aimed them at our kids yelling, "Get out now!" Children ran screaming and crying, and mama's came out to understand what was happening. They continued shouting at them to leave and evacuate now. They were told they had five minutes.

Many with no shoes, no toothbrushes, no clothes, and with food cooking ran to our front gate following orders to leave immediately. Where would they all go? How would they eat? Go to school? Bill had arrived in Haiti the day before and was just receiving calls about the eviction at Kay Anj. I was landing on an American Airlines flight as it was happening. We rented a small house near the airport that we would stay in when we came to Haiti. It had three bedrooms and one bathroom and was quite modest. It had an 8-foot wall with razor wire for security. We brought everyone to this small house. We locked all of our office supplies, computers, and printers in one bedroom to keep them safe. Our Kay Anj family would live in the two remaining bedrooms and use the one bathroom. It was a temporary solution and the only one we had.

The bathroom toilet stopped working on day four. I have no idea how everyone went to the bathroom for the 10 weeks they lived in the house. We had come in to attend our head mama, Adelines, nursing school graduation. She was graduating first in her class and we wouldn't have missed this opportunity to celebrate with her. After the ceremony we hosted 10 more of Adeline's wonderful family at the same house that now had 60 people living in it! What's 10 more for a night? It was a nice diversion to the fear, anger, and frustration that we were going through. After meeting with one highly-respected and highly-recommended attorney, who charged us $1,500 to look at our dossier to determine if he wanted to take our case, we felt confident we'd be home very soon. We were elated when he said he'd take our case.

We met twice at his office in Cap Haitien. We asked if he loved Jesus. He said yes so we prayed before our meetings. He appeared to be very uncomfortable. Then the communication ceased. No calls. No meetings. No documents. Nothing. We would go to his office and sit for hours until he showed up. He was visibly angry and told us he'd call us and not to come to his office. The very last time I went to his office I went to officially remove him as our attorney. I sat at his reception desk and in Haitian Kreyol, on a small napkin, wrote our letter of withdrawal from the case. We later had it officially documented and put in our dossier. We called everyone we knew in Cap Haitien for help. We even called Sophia Martelly, the wife of the Haitian President, Michel Martelly. She had heard about our situation from the Nouveliste newspaper that we put an article in. We were told to "make noise" so we made noise. Dame Martelly called our new attorney as we were sitting with him and told him to do whatever he needed to do to get us back in our homes. And with our second attorney we were told, "He will definitely get your family back in their homes."

We head to his office. He is smaller, thin, and unlike many Haitians, looks old for his age. He goes to work on our behalf and at the order of Sophia Martelly. Three weeks later we hear that they have agreed to let us go back to our homes. Thank you God! We pay his expensive bill but we are now home. From our second attorney we learn that as is common in Haiti, there is a family that says it's their land, because their family farmed it for over 50 years, not ours. We knew people this had happened to so we made sure we crossed every "T," and dotted every "I." Our 40 acres is owned by the Haitian government. We have a legal, 99-year lease with them. It took us three years to complete the process and the lease with the Haitian government.

How could they evict us when we don't own the land? The government is our landlord. Why aren't they helping us? During the 10 weeks away from our homes we continued the fight in Port au Prince. We went to the Director of the DGI and the Domain. All was legal on our end. The H family, as we call them, was given three dates to go to Port au Prince and show their legal documents that say they own the land and we need to leave. This is called the three-strike rule. They didn't show up for any of the three dates. We celebrated but celebrated a bit too soon. We found out that the documents were not on legal letterhead so we had to begin the three-strike process all over again. I was sure someone purposely did this to us.

We took our case to the highest court in Haiti. The Cour de Cassasion, or the Supreme Court. We were told it would be two to three years before a decision would be made. In March of 2016, I was sent a copy of a subpoena. It said that I was required to show up in the Cap Haitien Court of Appeals on March 18th. *What was this all about? Was I in trouble?* Our Haitian Director, Alan, told me I was fine and that I only needed to show my passport to the judge. But for what? Alan assured me I was fine and it was not a big deal. Bill and I flew to Cap Haitien the night before the 9 a.m. court hearing where I would just show my passport and then go home.

Something told me to talk to my friend, Istvan Papp, who is a leader in the UN in the North of Haiti. Istvan brought his friends, one who is a Haitian attorney, to dinner. Charnel, the attorney, asked to read our dossier. Bill, Istvan, Ashley, and I ate, chatted and were enjoying the evening. That's when all hell broke loose. Charnel had finished reading our very thick dossier, looked at me and said, "You're in a lot of trouble, Debbie." "Why?" "I just have to show my passport tomorrow morning, right?" "No, you have already been charged, tried, and convicted of three years in jail for spoliation. Bill and I sat stunned. We couldn't breathe. *What is spoliation? How did I get convicted without a trial? Am I going to jail...in Haiti?*

We sat until midnight discussing the plan and strategy for the trial at 9 a.m. the next morning. We learned that I was charged months prior to tampering with or destroying evidence involved in a legal case. They say on December 14, 2008, the day of our eviction, I came back wielding a machete and a gun. It is documented that I broke through the new lock the UDMO police placed on our gate. They say I then forcibly removed the unarmed guards they placed inside our Kay Anj village. I've been given the name Debbie Don't Play in Haiti but I have never wielded a machete or a gun. I immediately emailed and called the United States Embassy. I got a form letter in return. I then emailed the US Ambassador, Mr. Peter Mulrean, personally. He asked his assistant, Mr. Robert Hannan, to reply to my email. Mr. Hannan replied with the following email:

Dear Ms. Harvey,

As promised, I am responding again to your inquiry to Amb. Mulrean.

I can only re-emphasize our advice to leave Haiti now. We will not be able to intervene in the proceedings and as mentioned, it is possible the proceedings on March 22 will not be a transparent exercise in justice. We strongly advise that you leave the country now and allow your lawyer to represent you at the hearing. I cannot state strongly enough the need to avoid detention in a Haitian jail. If you are detained now and or in the future, as I mentioned, please do notify us immediately. The 24-hour switchboard will pass through a call to the duty office outside of working hours. The number is 509 22 29 80 00. We will make every effort to visit you in the first few days but our ability to provide services to a citizen in Cap Haitien will be limited. The email address is ACSPAP@state.gov.

We can only release information about you with your written permission. As an advance precaution, I am attaching a Privacy Act Waiver. If you wish, you may complete the form now and scan and send it to us at ACSPAP@state.

gov and we will use it to contact the persons you specify in the event you are detained.

Regards,

Robert F. Hannan, Jr.
Consul General,
Embassy of the United States of America
Port-au-Prince, Haiti

Everyone begged me to leave Haiti. Deb, you have a family in the U.S. Only one person told me to stay, Cathy Shaffer. She is my prayer warrior and spiritual mentor. She called me at 5 a.m. and said, "God's already won the battle, you need to stay and fight for your family." I did have a plan B exit strategy. I had an American friend who was working in the Dominican Republic. He was ready at the border, only 45-minutes from the courtroom, in case I was heading to prison and needed to flee quickly. Charnel suggested strongly that Bill go back home to the United States. He was sure that if the witnesses saw Bill in the court room they'd point him out and he could go to jail, too. It was better for just one of us to go to jail, not both of us. Bill, very reluctantly, agreed to go home. He was very concerned for me and my safety, but after much prayer together, he decided it was best if he left. We hugged for what felt like an hour. God brought two angels into my life that week. Both had a very specific purpose and they fulfilled God's role for them more beautifully and confidently than you could ever imagine.

Malia, a friend I graduated from high school with in 1982, came that week on her second trip to Haiti to help in our orphanage. She had no idea until she arrived all that was unravelling. Her husband, Jon, and daughter, Anna, were with her. Charnel suggested that Malia be my support in court each day. I asked her if she would go with me, I told her I had no idea what it meant for her or her family. It was very unnerving for Malia and Jon. Jon pulled me aside privately and asked if I could guarantee his families safety. I responded the only way I knew how at that moment, "I can't Jon." "I can't guarantee they'll be safe but I know God knows. God will protect us and the truth will be revealed." I have always believed that light shines in the darkness.

Malia sat in the back of the courtroom, behind my attorneys, every minute of the trial. She drew all that was going on and kept Bill updated with texts.

She was my support, my rock. Every time I would look back at her she would give me the biggest smile and two thumbs us. Translated, you're OK, Debbie. It's going to be OK. I sat in the Chez Jijman, or the Judgement Seat. I was already guilty and had already been convicted. I was not allowed to cross my legs and was told to always look at the faces of the judges. It was considered rude to take your eyes off the three judges. I had one dress that I wore regularly to meetings and appointments in Haiti. I sat in my "appointment" dress in a pool of sweat praying to the oversized crucifix above the heads of the judges.

The first day in court I was given one week to find an English-speaking interpreter, as it is an International Law that states that I am entitled to an interpreter that speaks my language. If I don't have one I will be given time to find one. I was referred to a woman named Denise. She was a friend of a friend and spoke French, Haitian Kreyol, and English. We met and I told her the details of my case and she agreed to be my English-speaking interpreter. Charnel wanted me to practice "provocation" before my court dates began. He wanted me, Denise, and Malia to go to his office and have his partners play the roles of the prosecuting attorneys, judges, and prosecutor. He would videotape each session so that he would know what I needed to work on. Denise was nowhere to be found. I called, texted, emailed, and called some more. No Denise. My first provocation session was in one hour and I had no interpreter. I went through my entire contact list calling everyone I knew looking for an interpreter who spoke both French and English. One of our kids, Nashi, sitting with me said, "Orano is here." "Where's Nashi?" I said. "He's in school." "Go get him out of his English class, please."

Orano had been our English teacher for just a month and loved working at Kay Anj. I asked Orano if he spoke French and after his "well, uh" I said, that's great, I need you. Can you come now to meet with my attorney for provocation? Orano had no idea what he was in for. His reply was, "Of course I will, if you need me." *I definitely need you, Orano.* Orano needed to get out of the car on the way to Charnels office and I was sure, just like Denise, he would disappear. To my surprise, he'd arrived before we did to Charnel's office. Charnel thought Orano was a thoughtful interpreter and was grateful for him, too. I called my new team my Ekip Jezi. They were my Jesus team.

After a week of provocation, going over proper responses and removing emotion, the trial would begin. It would be two, long weeks of lies, deception, and corruption. I learned that I'd been charged, tried, and convicted first because the family, and the attorneys using them, trying to say our land was theirs, did not receive a payout from us so they went after me personally. They made up the spoliation story to scare me so that I would give them a payout they'd not received yet. Our HHA board made a decision from day one that we would fight this biblically and legally right. Right in the eyes of God, our Haitian family, the country of Haiti and ourselves. We would be just as bad as the family bribing us if we paid them and succumbed to corruption. What would we be teaching our kids in Haiti? We would fight this honestly, we vowed.

And so I sat in the Chez Jijman praying Psalm 91 and Ephesians 6:10. The prosecuting attorneys brought their two witnesses in. One at a time they were asked to tell what they saw on December 14, 2014 at Kay Anj Village. They both described an angry group of men, all wanting to retaliate for our family having been evicted. They were our neighbors and we had a nice relationship. Their children attended our school and we built a clean-water well for them. They appreciated us. The witnesses were each asked if they saw the person in the courtroom who wielded the machete and the gun. Both said they did not. Just then, we believe out of desperation, the lead prosecuting attorney stood up over me, pointed his finger in my face and yelled, "You're a weed-smoking drunk who steals organs from street kids!" I didn't understand all he said as he spoke in French. I asked Orano what he said. He wouldn't tell me. He told me it wasn't nice and it didn't matter. I asked him again to tell me. "Deb, I'm not going to repeat it. It's not true so you don't need to know." I asked him for the last time to tell me. He realized that I was frustrated and I wasn't going to stop asking so he'd better tell me. I was saddened at what the attorney had said, but not surprised.

All three judges got up and swiftly left the courtroom. *Was I going to jail? What's happening? Why did they leave?* They returned 15-minutes later and told us that they'd walked out because they respect their court of law and the judicial process. They were very angry at what the attorney had said to me and they didn't want to say anything ugly in their courtroom so they made the decision to remove themselves. They asked the attorney to stand up next to me and apologize to me and all in the courtroom. Very sheepishly he said he was sorry for his comment. I knew I could be very angry and hate him or I could turn the other cheek. When we finished that day I decided to shake the hand of all three prosecuting attorneys. I wanted them to see that I was a kind, respectful, human being. Not the monster they were making me out to be. I reached my hand to the first attorney and he backed away. The other two shook my hand. I felt better. The final day in court ended with each side giving their reason for me to go to prison or not to go to prison. When both were finished I was told to leave the Chez Jijman and sit with my attorneys. I was petrified and unsure of what was coming next. My attorney leaned in close and whispered, "You're 99 percent free." *I'm free? It's over? Well, at least 99 percent over.*

I dropped to my knees with Malia, with tears flowing down both of our faces and thanked God for His protection. In the end it was all corruption. They wanted us to pay them for something that was not theirs. They thought they could scare us and threaten us into paying. 2 Timothy 1:7 says, "For I did not give you a spirit of fear, but of power, of love, and self-control." I repeated this over and over to myself. How do we deal with the corruption? We are in Haiti to love people, build relationships, and to help children. Can anything be done about corruption? The short answer is yes. Around the world, we find inspiring examples of cities and countries making progress in the fight against corruption. Not everywhere, to be sure, and even with these success stories, progress does not happen quickly. I believe corruption is similar to cancer. It finds its way into our organizations, and if we ignore it, it spreads. We need to act fast and remove the cancer or the corrupt person in our organization. If we don't, they will bring in friends and relatives and the cancer will continue to spread. The expectation is that they will continue to behave corruptly, whether that's lying or stealing. We must hold these people accountable. Ask for receipts, don't accept excuses. We're helping both of us when we have checks and balances. Accountability is measuring performance, listening to them, and allowing them to be heard.

Use your local police and/or public servants. They can often be a part of the problem, but when we ask them not to focus on individuals but the corruption itself, they appear to want to assist. The people of Haiti have long felt both abused and neglected by centralized control (both Haitian and foreign). The result may be a kind of learned-helplessness, which can lead to believing that it's OK to take from the "blans." Build relationships with your staff. Don't do anything for them that they can do for themselves. Love them and respect them. And, most importantly, listen to them and allow them the gift of your time. Allow them to be heard.

Chapter 5:

HIRING AND FIRING YOUR STAFF IN HAITI

> Proverbs 27:17: "Iron sharpens iron, and one man sharpens another."

IF YOU KNOW ANYONE LIVING OR WORKING IN HAITI, you've probably heard them lament about their issues with Haitian staff. From their managers to nannies, culturally hiring and firing is just not the same. Jobs and work are a family's livelihood. In Haiti, children die when their parents can't afford to buy food or pay for medications. With no job, children do not go to school in Haiti. Public school is not free, which means mom or dad must have income to pay for tuition. Because the unemployment rate hovers around 70 percent, finding a job is like hitting the lottery.

People will do and say anything to get hired. When we first started going to Haiti we hired a wonderful, trustworthy (or so we thought), honest man. We would send him our monthly funds for food, rent, and tuition for the children in our new orphanage. Little did we know that he was holding much of it, and with the pastor's wife down the street's help, they would purchase food for the kids, make only small amounts of food, and then sell the rest of the food and keep the money for themselves. We figured this out pretty quickly and we told him that we no longer needed his services. He was angry but he knew he'd been caught so he left and other than passing him on the street, we didn't see him much after that. We weren't so lucky with a few other employees.

We learned early on that all we ever wanted or needed to know is in the Code Du Travay. At the local labor offices they live and die by this book. We had been hiring, and in a few cases, firing improperly. We studied the Code du Travay and learned how to hire, provide proper employee contracts, and when necessary, fire the way Haiti wanted us to. We hired staff that we would have on payroll monthly, and we'd hire men and women from our local community for odd jobs that we would pay by the job. I make it sound very easy. It's not that simple. I've learned from my nine years working in Haiti, "Pa janm ase," or "it's never enough." In September of 2016, while renewing all of our employee contracts, four of our security guards decided they wanted a 46 percent pay raise. We typically give 5 to 6 percent raises each year determined by performance. I met with them a few times in person to listen to why they believed they should be given raises. I listened and listened. They believed the job they were doing should be valued higher and they should just be paid more. None of these men went to school. We provided them with two meals each day, their children attended our school, and we gave them uniforms and training. When I did not agree to give them raises they said they wouldn't sign their new contracts. I told them it was their choice, but that I was not firing them, they were making the decision to leave. They were as angry as I've ever seen grown men. They yelled and screamed at me so intensely that they were spitting everywhere. I called my attorney to come explain to them that they will have no job if they do not sign their contracts. They were given 24 hours to make the decision.

One of the men lived on-site with his wife and two children. They were house parents in addition to his security job. They had a nice home to live in, kids in our school, food, electricity, clean water, and more. He was gambling with his family's future. They could lose everything. The day before they were to sign the contracts they threatened me personally and said they'd "burn down our village with everyone in it." That was it for me. I would not live in fear of these men. I had to change hotels, and hire an armed guard to go with me everywhere. It was one of the first times in all my years in Haiti that I felt truly afraid. I sat in my hotel room, hives all over my body from stress, and I memorized 2Timothy 1:7: God did not give us a spirit of fear, but of power, love, and self-control. I admit that I was scared. I believe our guards were talking with and being advised by a former employee. I believe he was telling them to hold out for the money that we would most likely succumb to their demands (out of fear), and give them the raises. We didn't. It was time to sign their contracts. They all sat in a row as I handed the first guard his contract. He looked at each of the others, pen in one hand and contract in the other. He had fear in his eyes as he looked at the others. Then

I saw his wife with tears streaming down her face screaming from outside the room for him to sign the contract. She was yelling, "We'll lose everything, sign it!" They shook their heads and said no. He didn't sign the contract. One by one we went down the line. I handed them the contract and a pen, they didn't sign and I gently took the pen and contract back and said you've made your decision, thank you. When we were finished the four men stood up and began screaming again. All four at the same time. It was deafening. I had to get to the airport, but also had to create a document for the Labor Department informing them that the four guards had resigned effective today. As I walked away they continued to follow me screaming that it wasn't fair and they want their jobs. I calmly told them they'd made their decision. It was over, I thought. Thank God it was finally over.

That night when I arrived home I had messages on my phone from the four men begging for their jobs back. They said they were sorry and made a mistake. I truly felt sorry for them. They listened and took advise from someone they trusted. They believed they'd win, he told them they'd win. In the end they lost everything. In Haiti, when someone quits or is fired you pay them an amount determined by the formula in the Code du Travay. We paid them and have not heard from them since. Pa janm ase. It's never enough.

Our village is located on an old, dirt road off of the main road to the Dominican Republic. The community is called Decle. Decle is a very poor village with many people living in mud huts. Most are uneducated and all need work. When we signed the contract with the Haitian government for our beautiful piece of property, we promised to hire the local people for jobs that came available. We were happy to do this as we'd been intentional about becoming good neighbors. We respected them, brought a clean-water well in for them (they were walking miles for dirty water), and put it right in the middle of their community. When we were evicted by the UDMO police they defended us and fought for us. It was a mutually, beneficial relationship. Then one day it turned ugly. We were driving down the dirt road through Decle and the faces of our friends on the street were angry as they watched us drive down to our village. We were stopped just before our entrance by burning tires and somewhere between 25-30 men wielding machetes and screaming. This was something we weren't used to. Bill and I got out of the car (we had a few volunteers with us, too), and with the help of our driver, Harry, asked the men what the problem was. Yelling and screaming ensued, and we couldn't understand any of them as they all yelled over each other. We learned that they just wanted jobs. They wanted to be allowed in our gates to cut grass with their machetes. We asked who the leader was and they all pointed to a tall, thin man with a quiet, kind face. He did not look angry like the others.

Daniel would make a list of 10 men that could come in today and work for the day. They could work for four days and we'd pay them at the end of the fourth day. This calmed them, and they removed the burning tires and allowed us to enter our village. For today they were OK with our agreement. Months later the same thing happened again, but this time there were threats to our mama's and employees who walked on the road to go home at the end of each day. They tore down and burned our sign that was on the main road. One man pulled a knife on our laundry mama, Nadege, and she told him to get that thing out of her side and talk with his mouth if he wanted to talk to her. The very next day I went to the courthouse and filed "mandas" on four men that I had heard were the ones responsible for the manifestation. These were legal restraining orders. If any one of the four men was seen near our village they would immediately be thrown in jail. After much prayer, calls to people we know living in Haiti, and those who have been working with Haitian staff, we decided to have a town-council meeting.

The following Sunday at 3 p.m., 40 not-so-happy people showed up to our meeting. We asked the police to come just in case things went sideways. We asked them why they burned our sign, kept us from being able to leave, and threatened our family. They said we haven't given enough jobs to the people in the Decle community. I let them know that we currently have 15 people from Decle on our payroll. The man said that he's not working here. And then it hit me, if we don't have YOU on our payroll then we have no one from your village on our payroll. All he was concerned about was him. Just him and his family. They were also very angry about the mandas and wanted me to remove them. I told them I would remove them when there was peace and respect on the street. I have not removed them as of today. That's when I learned that no matter what we do it will never be enough. Pa janm ase.

At the town-council meeting, we asked all 40 to vote on three community leaders. Our plan was to meet with these leaders weekly to talk about what's going on in the community. The community MUST be a part of the solution. They know where the corruption is and they know how it works. We make the rules for our leaders, and those coming in to work with us, very clear, which enables discretion. When we need to get info to the families, we now contact the leaders. They liked this idea. To ensure peace in our neighborhood, and with the leaders support, we decided to hire 10 men per month to cut our grass with machetes. We told them we'd bring in five men on the first of each month, and five men on the 15th. Each group works for five days and earns $50 at the end of their job. The leaders are in charge of giving us the list of the men working each month. Will this create jealousy among those living in the community? Yes, it most likely will. Good things usually do because human beings tend to be petty and don't want to see others have more success or money than they do. Whatever you do is probably going to create some jealousy unless absolutely everybody benefits from it. And that's not going to happen, especially here, so let's all agree that we will never be able to make everyone happy. Pa janm ase. The men that are chosen that week sign a Temporary Employee contract, and we take a photo and file it just in case something happens while they're working for us. It's been working well for months now. All is peaceful on our street, for now.

Now let's talk about trust and honesty in those we hire. This is a very tough subject, as I love Haiti and her people. We are Americans (or Canadians, French, German, Asian) and we will never understand the deep, deep roots of the Haitian culture. Unfortunately, we have trained the Haitian people to beg at the airports, to not show up to work when we give them a job, and to lie to us. We are blans (foreigners). It is believed that we have a lot of money and we won't miss just a little if it goes missing. Some turn a blind eye and think, "It was only a couple bucks and I'm sure he or she needed it." If we continue this thinking the cycle of poverty will just keep spinning in Haiti. We are perpetuating that cycle by not holding our staff accountable. We build a relationship with them, we love them, they work for us, and we need to believe in them enough to hold them accountable. Some believe by telling an employee they have to be accountable for our money, it is our nice way of saying, "You need to prove to me that you did what I wanted you to do with this money." It's our fancy way of saying, "I don't trust you." Unfortunately for me personally, having been taken, lied to, and stolen from, I am jaded. I admit it. I love the Haitian people with every fiber of my being, but I'm jaded.

My rule of thumb with staff is innocent until proven guilty. That may be wrong, and a lot of you may not agree with me, but it works for me. One man came to our town-council meeting so angry that he wouldn't even sit down. He stood, leaning on a wall, his face crunched-up and seething. He was very angry at us. He couldn't wait for the meeting to begin so he could start spewing his hate for us. After listening to him for a few minutes and realizing he wasn't going to stop, we asked the police to escort him out of our village. Again, he was livid. We later learned that he was the brother of one of our four guards that had resigned. We came up with a plan, and what we thought was a very good one. Obviously, we couldn't hire either of the brothers, but they were influential in the Decle community. People listened to them and followed their lead. We needed them on our side. So, we gave their mother a job. Bernadine does the laundry when we have volunteer groups come to stay at Kay Anj. She was thrilled. We didn't hear anything from the boys, but we knew that if we gave their mother a job it would calm them down, as they would now have money coming into their house. In the end, our goal, mission, and hope is that we become an organization completely run and managed by Haitians. It sounds odd, but if we could leave Haiti knowing that over the years our Haitian leadership had been trained to manage Kay Anj in a Christ-like, loving, and honest way, then we all win.

We've talked about hiring Haitian staff, now let's look at the best way to hire American missionaries and staff. After putting three different Haitian men in the position of Manager of Operations in Haiti, we learned that we simply needed an American to be present to work with our Haitian manager. We would work toward complete sustainability, but for now we needed an American's presence. We began the tough task of finding missionaries (we wanted a married couple to model for our children) who wanted to answer God's call on their lives and move to Haiti to manage our orphanage, school, farming, and church. We interviewed a handful of people who responded to our ad on a Christian, missionary site. We skyped, and paid for a short trip to Haiti so we could meet them in person and see how they interact with our Haitian family. They were wonderful, loving, and happy to be in Haiti with our Kay Anj family. They decided to sell everything, their home, cars, and belongings and head to Haiti to be our directors.

For some reason, soon after arriving and settling in, things changed. They wanted more control, and they didn't agree with the way we were doing things. We determined with both couples (two years apart) that we had philosophical differences that were not known before their move to Haiti. Because we failed-forward twice, I decided to move to Haiti for an extended period of time. What were we missing when interviewing missionaries? I learned that people can have it all together. They can speak eloquently. They can have deep wisdom, experience in all the necessary places, and faith that moves mountains. We can give everything away. But, if we don't have sacrificial, humble love, Paul says in 1Corinthians 13:3: "If I give all that I possess to the poor and give over my body to hardship that I may boast, but do not have love, I gain nothing." I'm not saying they didn't love our kids or our mama's, papas, and staff. I'm saying we need American directors or managers who walk humbly, and as we always say at HHA, exude a Christ-like and honest love.

Chapter 6:

EDUCATION IS FREEDOM

"I will instruct you and teach you in the way you should go; I will counsel you with my loving eye on you." -Psalm 32:8

EDUCATION IS FREEDOM, ESPECIALLY IN HAITI. HAITI'S abysmal educational system remains an obstacle to building the expertise and skills needed to help this impoverished country recover for the next generation, and generations to come. Children in Haiti are being deprived of a quality education. The Haitian education system is lacking in all aspects. How do you find a curriculum that will provide your kids the education that will allow them to succeed in University and be the future leaders for Haiti?

The enrollment rate for primary school, and preschool through 6th grade, is 88 percent. Secondary schools, 7th-12th grades, enroll 20 percent of eligible-age children. Higher education is provided mostly by universities in Port au Prince and Cap Haitien. The Haitian education system follows the leadership of the Ministre de l'Éducation Nationale et de la Formation Professionnelle (MENFP). The Ministry provides very little funds to support public education. As a result, the private sector has become a substitute for governmental-public investment in education as opposed to adding to it. The Ministry is limited in its ability to improve the quality of education in Haiti.

The children in the Haitian Education System produce the lowest total rate in the education realm of the Western Hemisphere. Haiti's literacy rate of about 61 percent is far below the 92 percent average literacy rate for Latin American and Caribbean countries. Studies show that only 10 percent of Haitian children who enter the first grade will complete school. Haiti faces shortages in educational supplies and qualified, trained teachers. Research shows that less than 10 percent (some studies say as low as 3 percent) of the country's 10 million people speak French fluently, and in most schools, even the teachers don't understand it very well, although they're asked to teach it. As a result, most Haitian children are never given the opportunity to become fluent readers. They never learn to read well, so they can't read to learn.

Private schools (run by U.S., Canadian, and French organizations) and schools run by churches educate approximately 90 percent of all students in Haiti. Enrollment in Primary school is approximately 88 percent. Haiti's Secondary schools enroll just at 20 percent. Higher education is provided by universities and other public and private institutions and enrollment is less than 1 percent of young people. Should schools be taught in Haitian Kreyol, their native tongue, or in French? Studies have proven that students learn best in the language that they speak and understand best. The language in which information is disseminated is very important, not only for learning, but also for creativity and innovation.

Lekòl Kominotè Matènwa (LKM), a school in La Gonave, Haiti, shows that Haitian children who are taught in their native tongue, Haitian Kreyòl, achieve much higher scores than their counterparts who learn in French. Once children have a strong foundation in their native language, they are substantially better equipped to learn all school subjects, including French and English as second languages. In 2014, all 25 sixth-graders at LKM passed Haiti's official National Exam administered by the state. Only 71 percent passed the test nationally. What's less measurable, but profoundly important, is the dignity of these children, whose joyful creativity is set free when they can learn in their native Kreyòl. What you need to know and is vitally important is that these 25 students took the sixth-grade, National Exam in French, not in Haitian Kreyol. To be successful as a bilingual speaker in Haiti the children must learn to read and understand Haitian Kreyol as the language of instruction in preschool through grade four. French, and in many cases, French and English, should be taught as foreign language from grade four on. You can purchase bilingual textbooks online.

When we were in the process of building our school in 2014, we began looking at and researching the Haitian education system. We studied the test results, graduation rates, and determined that teaching our kids in Haitian Kreyol would be a priority and a gift. We also knew we would come up against many Haitian people who would disagree. French is the language of the educated and the wealthy, why would we NOT teach in French? We were right, as most parents, newly-hired teachers, and local officials told us that we must provide the children with a French curriculum. We didn't agree so we headed to the small island of La Gonave. My friend, Dona, a teacher for 30 years, and I made plans with Chris Low, founder of Matenwa Community Learning Center, to learn about her methodology and Haitian Kreyol curriculum that were so successful. La Gonave is off the coast of Port au Prince and is sometimes called the "forgotten island." It is very hard to get to; we flew to Port au Prince and then took a puddle-jumper where we landed on the beach on LaGonave. We then had to ride in a pickup truck for two hours up a dry river bed. We finally arrived and were greeted by Joelle who would show us where we would be staying for a few days. We lived with a wonderful family who warmly welcomed us. In all of our years coming to Haiti we'd never lived with a family in their home. We were excited yet also apprehensive. It was definitely an adventure and we loved every minute.

We walked a short distance from the house to the school we would be spending most of our time in. We wanted to truly understand the Matenwa Methodology. We believed it would be best for our students, too, but needed to know all so that we could bring it home and implement it in our Kay Anj Village School. And so for days Dona and I observed in the classroom, attended staff meetings, met with teachers individually, and spent time with students. We saw firsthand how the Matenwa Methodology was encouraging a love of learning in these children. The kids arrived early to school and many stayed late. They wanted to learn. We took pages of notes and went back down the mountain, this time on the back of a motorcycle, and started the process for bringing the Matenwa Methodology to Lekol Harvey. We came back and immediately went to work. We learned about a Professional Teacher College in Cap Haitien. Lecole Nomal was a catholic, coed college that provided the students with a three-year, teaching degree at graduation. We made appointments to interview teachers. We needed to hire six teachers and a Directress (principal). We were well-prepared with interview questions and applications in Haitian Kreyol.

We were looking for younger teachers who were eager for change in the Haitian education system. We wanted teachers who had never taught but who were educated in teaching. The Matenwa methodology is different for Haiti and we wanted to find teachers who could think outside the box. We brought the seven teachers we agreed on back for a second interview. We asked how they felt about not teaching in French, but teaching all subjects in Haitian Kreyol. They stared at each other for a few seconds. No one wanted to be the first to speak. We asked if they'd ever heard of Matenwa or Michel DeGraff? We explained that Michel DeGraff is a professor of linguistics at MIT in the United States and is a native of Haiti. He is working with the Ministry of Education to get all schools in Haiti to be taught in their native tongue, Haitian Kreyol. The stares continued. Our teachers had been taught in French and their Lecole Normal taught all classes in French. Why would we want to teach in Haitian Kreyol? We explained and showed them the research findings. When you use Haitian Kreyol as the primary language of learning you can make the learning truly *active* for your students. They began to nod their heads and get excited about the prospects of this new (to them) methodology.

We then asked them how they felt about corporal punishment. You see, in most schools in Haiti, disciplining the children physically is expected. Matenwa disagrees and so do we. We will have a zero-tolerance rule for corporal punishment. Children will not kneel on the floor for hours as is common in Haiti. We were shocked and saddened when we learned that all of our children had been physically disciplined at the school they were attending. At our family meeting, just before our new school was to open, I was trying to make a point about the dangers and humiliation of corporal punishment. I asked the children who'd been hit or whipped at school to raise their hands. I was sure of three or four, but had no idea every child's hand would go up. Tears filled my eyes though they didn't know. Even our five-year-olds got whipped? Yes, they did. I promised them that this would not happen in our new Lekol Harvey. There would be discipline, of course, but appropriate and fair discipline. We held our school registration in August of 2014. We met many times and felt well-prepared for registration day. We knew the parents and families would have many questions for us. We were not prepared to learn that of the 53 families who came to apply with their child, not one could read or write. We were stunned. We thought we'd have a few that wouldn't be able to read the application so we had people ready to help them. But, we had no idea and were not prepared when all 53 asked for help reading and completing their child's application. Our hope is that the children learning to read in our school will go home and help their parents learn how to read. As we get ready to open our doors for our fourth year at Lekol Harvey, we are excited about the possibilities for our students. Learning in Kreyol, and introducing STEM education, the sky's the limit for these kids!

Thanks to Michel DeGraff and Chris Low, in July of 2015, Haiti's government announced a new policy that states schools must educate students in Haitian Kreyòl, the native language of Haitians, rather than French, the language traditionally used in schools. This is the first agreement between Haiti's Ministry of National Education and Professional Training and the newly-created Haitian Creole Academy (AKA). AKA was inaugurated in December of 2014. AKA's mandate includes the establishment of conventions using the

Haitian Kreyòl and the promotion of Kreyòl in all sectors of society. The core objective of this new agreement between MENFP and AKA is to further promote Kreyòl, and Kreyòl speakers' linguistic rights. MENFP and AKA have now created a formal framework to work together to expand the use of Kreyòl as a teaching tool at all levels of Haiti's system, from kindergarten to University. This also entails the standardization of Kreyòl writing, and the training of teachers for instruction of, and in, Kreyòl.

We must now include sciences, and math can play a pivotal role toward that end. It should not be acceptable for students to receive the equivalent of a high school diploma and never actively participate in a laboratory experiment. How should it be considered learning if students are forced to memorize math problems for state exams? The culture of education in Haiti must change. STEM or science, technology, engineering and math, we believe, are the best kinds of active learning for our students. Learning science and math requires a great deal of reasoning, collaboration, and communication. In Haiti, such active learning, especially the interactive part, cannot be done in French because they do not speak French fluently. In Haiti and in Lekol

Harvey, it is only in Kreyòl that the majority of students can truly participate in interactive learning.

STEM learning is being heavily encouraged around the globe. According to the United Nations, "Capacity in science and technology is a key element in economic and social development." Encouraging STEM growth in Haiti can serve as a means to train future leaders within the professions of science, technology, engineering, and mathematics, as well as provide access to good jobs in Haiti. We are thrilled to announce that we have partnered with Lets Go Boys and Girls of Baltimore, Maryland. Let's Go Boys and Girls, founded by Clark "Corky" Graham, says the Let's Go mission is to inspire and support underserved students to become STEM professionals. Our teachers are being trained in STEM education this summer and we will kick off our STEM curriculum when our school opens for its fourth year in September of 2017. Corky believes that while there is a deficit of students entering STEM fields, the gap is most significant for the underserved, and for girls. To prepare our students to succeed in STEM, we need to not only spark their interest in STEM, but also to offer the support and encouragement to persevere in a STEM education. The educational transformation that needs to take place in Haiti will give the STEM subjects their rightful place in each school's curriculum. A culture of critical thinking must replace rote memorization, and full-learning immersion in the native language, Kreyol, can only boost the creativity and liveliness in the classroom of Haitian students.

We believe that in order to accomplish this dream of making Haiti an emerging country within the next decade and decades to come, STEM education, along with added emphasis in arts and languages, are vital in the classroom. Haitian students must learn to become creators, inventors, entrepreneurs, and noble citizens and devout mothers and fathers passing this love of learning on to their children and future generations. We believe that like all children, Haiti's children deserve to be happy and the right to dream. Right now most Haitian children are born into a life of physical work in the fields, or in city slums. For more than 50 percent of them, going to school is not a reality because they cannot afford the cost of tuition. Entrance fees, uniforms, books, semester fees, test fees, and a daily meal absorbed in the stomach in order for information to be absorbed in the brain, are all beyond these children's reach.

Our simple but profound belief is that Haitian schools should not feel like a punishment, but rather a fun, safe, peaceful, and creative learning environment. We believe that our school is a place where our children are absorbing knowledge because they are reading, hearing, and discussing information in their native language, Kreyol. It's the language that they understand and speak at home. At the same time, our children are learning a second and third language, French and English. If a child's first experience of reading is actually the "reading" of sounds without any understanding of the actual vocabulary, as Haitian linguist Ives Dejean points out, this impedes a child's ability to learn either language well. Education is the most effective way out of poverty. It is assuredly one of the best ways to end poverty, deprivation, crime, and deceit.

Chapter 7:

HUMBLY AND EFFECTIVELY SERVING THE POOR – EVERY TIME I LEAVE I KNOW LESS.

"And what does the Lord require of you but to act justly, to love mercy, and to walk humbly with your God." -Micah 6:8

MY FLIGHT TO CAP HAITIEN WAS FULL OF WELL-INTENTIONED Americans. I had learned in my years of travel and time spent in Haiti that donations, free aid, and unguided volunteerism often creates dependence. I knew that helping blindly often does more harm than good. A flight full of Americans eager to fix Haiti and save the helpless locals was not good.

Poverty is on display constantly in the news. It's as far away as a distant continent and as close as your local city. But the sheer magnitude of the problem can overwhelm and paralyze you if you don't see beyond poverty as an issue and get to know poor people themselves. When you build relationships with people living in poverty, you'll begin to see that you can fight the monster of poverty by making a difference in individual lives.

In seeking to do justice for the weak, the fatherless, the afflicted, and the destitute, this requires great wisdom, prayerful reflection, and the development of intentional strategies. After many (and I mean many) mistakes made when we first started making trips to Haiti in 2008, we began to pray and ask ourselves and God some deep questions about how we were serving the poor and IF we were truly helping them. We wanted to do better. We wanted to learn more. How do we really help? We made all the classic mistakes. We thought we knew better, we gave handouts, we passed out candy, we brought in supplies, and we built surface relationships.

Today, I travel to Haiti at least once a month and spend a few months early each year. A couple of years ago I realized each time I left Haiti that I'd learned something during my trip that I knew nothing about.

I would arrive home and immediately research, seek council, and learn about this new subject. Every time I'd leave I'd know less. We are a Christian organization but we are not of the mindset that we need to be knocking on doors to bring people to Jesus. We have always believed that when we are authentic people will see Jesus in us. I have witnessed with my own eyes, a group of volunteers from a church in the United States, walk down our street meeting mothers, fathers, and children. They spend a few minutes with these beautiful people "getting to know them." They then ask them if they know Jesus. The Haitian people have been here so they know how to reply. "Well, we go to church." The church group feels a fire in their bellies. They are going to bring these families to Christ. Hallelujah! They talk to them about salvation, Jesus dying on the cross for their sins, and then they ask them if they want to ask Jesus into their hearts. "Yes, of course we do!" they all say. The well-meaning and loving church group then walks them through the prayer of salvation, maybe gives them a small gift (bible, cross) and they leave the home to head to the next family in need of salvation. As they work their way down the street and are joyfully getting into their van to leave, what they don't see is the Haitian families that were just "saved" laughing at them. It's the third time this month the same families have been "saved." They know the gig. They've had a lot of practice. They know exactly what the church group wants to hear. The church group then posts on their Facebook page that while in Haiti for a week they brought 27 people to Jesus. Again, Hallelujah!

Please don't misunderstand me. I am not saying we shouldn't go to Haiti and talk about Jesus, but because the people of Haiti have been through this so many times and for so many years I believe it's best and more effective to allow them to see Jesus in your everyday life with them. Why in the world would you think that someone you've known for 10 minutes would trust you enough to allow you to bring them to Jesus? And truthfully, the faith of the Haitian people far surpasses anything I've seen in the United States. They LOVE Jesus already. Yes, there are still some people that would benefit from learning about the grace and love of Jesus, but most grew up developing a deep relationship with Him. Why do we assume that because they are poor and in need that they don't know Jesus? Spend time in their communities building mutually-respectful relationships, and at the right time, the topic of Jesus will come up. You will talk for hours about Him because they already know Him. Rather than just jumping into an effort to serve poor people, ask God to direct you to focus on the specific people He wants you to help.

Don't approach service in Haiti with your own agenda; invite God to show you what He is already doing in poor people's lives and how you can participate in that work. Serve with intentional collaboration.

We clearly recognize that God was at work in our small village and local communities long before we began serving there. We seek to collaborate with people of different religious backgrounds (including voodoo). We recognize there are many ongoing, vibrant expressions of Kingdom ministry in which we encourage people to participate. May we, by God's grace, respond prayerfully, responsibly, and lovingly in serving the poor in our communities in Haiti.

Clauvis worked as a security guard with us from 2008 until he passed away in 2016. Clauvis' primary role on his job description was Prayer Warrior. At noon every day you would find our tall, thin, fragile Clauvis with arms raised to heaven, praying for each child and staff member by name. When Clauvis was a guard at the small, two-story home we rented as our orphanage for a few years, he was perfectly capable of handling all security matters that presented themselves. When we moved to our 40-acre village with 10 children's homes, a school, and a church, we knew he would not be able to guard the front gate as he had in the past. We knew we couldn't let him go as he and his family needed his monthly pay to survive. So, we made him "inside security." He would keep things safe inside and around our kids' homes. He was very happy with his new role.

I noticed Clauvis getting thinner than he already was in early 2016. We helped him get to the doctor a few times as he was told he had a stomach blockage. The medicine he was given wasn't working. I was at home in Virginia when I got a call asking if I'd send money for blood for Clauvis. I had no idea what that meant but trusted that it was necessary. When I arrived the next week to Kay Anj and saw Clauvis, I stopped and had to take a breath. He looked like a walking skeleton. I hugged him and said, "Oh, Clauvis, how are you?" He stepped back, grabbed my hand and said, "Deb, it's OK. Don't be sad for me. I'm going to be with Jesus soon." With tears in my eyes I hugged him and kissed him on his cheek. I was able to visit him in the hospital days before he passed away. His wife, I later learned was just a neighbor, was shoving all of his hospital bills in my face. You need to pay these, she said over and over. I asked her to leave as I was here to see Clauvis. When I left I paid the hospital for some of the expenses, but not all. She was not happy. Clauvis died the first time (I'll explain) when I got a phone call from our head mama, Adeline, saying Clauvis is at peace. He's gone. I was sad, but also knew Clauvis was free of pain and as he said, he was dancing with Jesus now. I was told his two, adult sons would meet me at our village the next day. They didn't say what they wanted, but I knew. They wanted me to pay for funeral arrangements. As soon as I arrived I was told that Clauvis didn't really die. His friends and family told me he did so that they could get some money from me for the funeral. I couldn't believe what I was hearing. Would people really do this? Yes, they would. I met with the sons, who were clearly grieving, and asked what they wanted. When they sadly said that they need money to pay for their dad's funeral, I promptly replied, "What funeral? Clauvis didn't die." They looked at each other with panic on their faces. I decided to be humble and kind. I told them that I knew that their dad didn't die yesterday and to kindly leave our village now. I thanked them and told them to have a nice day. They turned and quietly left. Ten days later, Clauvis died and this time for real. Again, the family asked us to pay for the funeral. I told them that Clauvis is in heaven now and that the funeral is for them. I didn't give them any money for the funeral and I didn't attend. I think about precious Clauvis often. He was a beautiful angel. I could have been angry with his "wife" and sons but I wasn't. It would have been wrong to pay for the funeral. It would have made us look like the hero and we are not. Passion and compassion are wonderful, but if we don't couple it with education, cultural respect, a curiosity for growth, and most importantly, a true desire to learn, then we're going to face many failures.

In today's model of missions, many well-meaning people are starting humanitarian organizations that work in the fields of sex trafficking, clean-water wells, orphanages, and social entrepreneurship. Haiti desperately needs help, but at the end of the day it appears that we're doing more harm than good if we think our volunteers matter more than the people we've set out to serve. Before the 2010 earthquake, Haiti grew a lot of good, nutritious rice. Actually, Haiti produced enough food to provide for itself and feed all of its people. But after the earthquake, aid began pouring in from all over the world. People, churches, and governments sent medicine, shelter, and food. Most of the food that was shipped in was free food. These well-meaning people coming to help the Haitian people were able to help for only a very, short time, but in the long run they put Haiti's rice farmers out of business. The local rice farmer can't compete with free rice so no one is buying his/her rice. After the crisis is over, the Americans, who look like hero's after bringing in all of the free rice move on, leaving ruined farms and farmers with nothing and no way to feed their families in their wake. The locals go back to doing business with the local farmer, but he already went out of business a while ago. Now, there isn't any rice. No free rice anymore and their friend who sold rice isn't selling, either.

We Americans did much more harm than good, and what's worse is that we didn't even realize we were doing it. At HHA we build relationships, ensuring that our work creates dignity, not dependency. By working with those who have been serving in Haiti long before us, and those who will be working in Haiti long after us, we can be sure our work is helping and not hurting. Before you get on a plane, or donate a pile of old clothes, ask the experts what Haiti really needs right now. Collecting and sending donations of clothes, food, and toys will put local merchants out of business. All the help that you want to provide can and should be done with monetary donations. Find smaller organizations who have a proven track record. These groups are your hands and feet, working where you want to work. Even just a $5 donation to an organization that you trust will do so much more good than you can imagine.

Without careful thought, we often provide aid that produces dependency and crushes the local economy. Our good intentions can have unintended, dire consequences. We fly off on mission trips to poor, impoverished villages, hearts full of pity and suitcases bulging with coloring books and beanie babies, trips that one Haitian leader and friend of mine describes as effective only in turning our people into beggars. Please hear me, I am in no way discouraging groups from going on mission trips. In fact, quite the opposite. We encourage Americans to go and serve and learn and be changed. We bring in five groups each year. What I am saying is that we all should truly think about why we are going and what we will do when we seek to help and serve the poor. Our free food and clothing distribution encourages ever-growing handout lines, diminishing the dignity of the poor while increasing their dependency. If a well-meaning group of people came into my community for the week to follow my kids around picking up after them, playing with and spoiling them, giving them toys, food, clothes and money, I would be very mad and frustrated. Maybe, I'd smile and say thank you, but then I would begin working to undo the damage they'd created. We should decide to empower and support communities as they work to get back on their feet. If we really want to help we need to ask what are the true needs of the community? If we really want to help, we must understand and know that we will be involved on a long-term basis, deeply and consistently engaging with our local communities. We need to listen to and learn the culture, understand the beliefs, respect their plans already moving and working. We need to recognize the gifts, the talents, and the sacrifices many have already made. We need to come alongside to support and love and help make their dreams come true. Not ours.

How do we effectively help our Haitian friends find contentedness? I believe we need to give them jobs. Work is livelihood. Work provides dignity. Work feeds families and pays for school tuition. Let's give them the proverbial hand-up rather than handout. Giving them moral support, and showing heart-felt humility and respect makes them aware that someone really does care about them and wants to improve their living conditions. By providing them with the opportunities to work, which will improve their living condition on their own, would increase self-esteem and help them overcome struggles they face every day. We work with the poor and needy to help them discover their own capabilities and God-given talents by giving them work at the right place and right time. Support them and let them know that they are of value and have gifts that God has blessed them with which can be used for meeting their basic needs and providing for their families. Approach your ministry efforts humbly. It's our responsibility as a sending organization to prepare, train, and educate our volunteers. We must understand and trust that God EXPECTS us as the sending organization to make ambassadors for Haiti of our mission-trip volunteers. We must teach them why we don't handout money. They need to understand why we don't bring in tons of toys, coloring books, and candy. They should learn the basics of the Haitian Kreyol language before coming. We need to teach them about the Haitian culture before they put their first foot on the ground in Haiti. They need to understand the problem of Restavek, the rules of the government in Haiti. Most importantly, they need to learn how to serve in love, and not hurt while helping. We tell them that while we want them to have a wonderful experience during their week at Kay Anj, this trip is not about them. You paid a lot of money, you took time off work, and you left your families, but this trip is not about you. It's about our Kay Anj family. You will be living with them for a week. You will love, respect, and build relationships with them. It's about them, not you.

Our volunteers often ask, "People ask me everyday what projects we'll be doing and what they can collect for me to bring to the kids and parents at Kay Anj." We let them know that at HHA we do not do projects. We don't build buildings, we build people and relationships. We believe that when projects become more important than people we lose focus on what God has us doing. And we do not bring in anything that we can purchase in Haiti. We will not put Haitian people out of business because well-meaning Americans wanted to feel good as they collected sunglasses, shoes, and coloring books. We make very clear to our volunteers that they are the face of HHA. They are the first person people see when they are introduced to HHA in Haiti or in the U.S. We hope that we make respectful, educated, always-learning, humble ambassadors for Haiti. When projects become more important than people we lose focus on what God has us doing. It's easy to feel overwhelmed by the needs of volunteers or employees in addition to the needs of the people you are trying to serve. And yet, studies have shown that investing in a solid, thriving, strategic plan will result in happier, healthier staff, mission-trip volunteers, and greater productivity as an organization. Recognize too, that God values poor people just as much as He does you, and in fact, He identifies especially with the poor. Realize that you can learn as much from poor people as they can learn from you. Ask God to give you the character (not just the skills) that you need to live and work among the poor effectively. Allow the poor people you serve to serve you by helping you grow more spiritually and emotionally mature. Love unconditionally, understand that some poor people are not always nice, and many will not appear to be worthy, deserving, or respectful, yet God calls us to love them no matter what. Remember that Jesus stopped for poor people in need, even if they were unpleasant. Ask God to help you reach out to all poor people He puts in your path. Invite God to let His unconditional love for them to flow through you into their lives. Allow them to see Jesus in you and all those who are the face of your organization.

> In Philippians 2:3–4 Paul said, "Let nothing be done through selfish ambition or conceit, but in lowliness of mind let each esteem others better than himself. Let each of you look out not only for his own interests, but also for the interests of others."

Chapter 8:

THE IMPORTANCE OF CONTACTS

"And my God will supply every need of yours according to his riches in glory in Christ Jesus."
-Phillipians 4:19

WE WERE DESPERATE AND TIRED OF FIGHTING. OUR family of 65 was living in a house with only one bathroom and two bedrooms. We met with a very prominent Haitian businessman, Mr. LaRoche, who told us to "make some noise." He said you have to take your situation public. Tell everyone that will listen. Get it in LeNouvelliste, it's the paper everyone in Haiti reads. I'm pretty good at making noise. You could call it a gift. I was told to find the well-know journalist, Cyrus Sibert. He lives in Port au Prince, but if you get his contact info he will listen to you. And so I went to the local restaurant, Lakay, where people go to be seen and to see others. I was talking with a good friend and asking if she knew Mr. Sibert. She nodded and said he's standing at the bar. *He was here? In Cap Haitien?* Here I go to make noise. I tried not to interrupt Mr. Sibert's conversation, but after standing on the outskirts of his group of friends for a few minutes I finally introduced myself. I told him that I'd been told to contact him and asked if he had a few minutes to hear my story. He told me to continue. I gave him the Reader's Digest version and he told me he would definitely put it all in the LeNouvelliste. He grabbed his phone from his pocket, called a Mr. Maxineau, who is a local reporter from Cap Haitien. Mr. Sibert told me to go now to meet Mr. Maxineau on 18th and L streets. "Now, right now?" "Yes, he's waiting for you," he said.

Jean, our Haitian manager at the time, and I got in our truck and left for the reporter's office. It was not my plan to be out after dark. I am usually back in my hotel room before dinner time. We sat on the side of the road, in our truck, waiting for Mr. Maxineau. Fifteen minutes later he came and got in the back seat of our truck. It felt like a movie. A bit of a scary movie at that. In the dark, at night, we told him all about our legal battle for our land. The injustice, the corruption, all of the dirty details. He told us exactly what he needed and that he needed it all, including photos by 8 a.m., so that it could get in the next edition of the paper. And then we paid him, in cash, and he left our car and went back to his office. We worked all night writing our report, digging for the best photos. True to his word, our article was in the next edition of LeNouvelliste. We received a few calls from people offering to help.

As we tirelessly fought for our beautiful, Kay Anj homes we finally found the contact we needed at the DGI (office in charge of land, taxes, etc.) who would listen to our plea. We told Mr. Morlan, Director of the DGI in Port au Prince, that we do not own our land. The Haitian government owns it and they should be fighting for us. We are just a tenant with a lifelong lease on our property. We did everything legally, everything we were required to do. We were given Mr. Toussaint to work with. He is a DGI attorney whose office is in Port au Prince. On his first trip up to Cap Haitien to meet with us I hugged him and sincerely thanked him for his help. I look back at that now and chuckle. Mr. Toussaint continued to come to Cap Haitien from Port au Prince on our dime, to "fight" for us. Nothing ever moved forward. We heard over and over, "just be patient, they'll go to jail." It's now two years later and we are only a bit further than we were when we started. We now know Mr. Toussaint strung us along to get trips and hotels paid for by us. Another BIG fail-forward for us. We continue to learn as we are tested. Now it was time to make noise and meet with people in powerful positions in Cap Haitien.

We were given the name of the Mayor of Cap Haitien from our friend and hotel owner, Nic Bussenius. We headed to the Mayor's office, where after waiting for two hours, we met Mr. Yvon Alteon. Yvon was much bigger than most Haitian men I knew. He was kind and pleasant and offered to help us in any way he could. He gave us the contact information for his boss, the Delegue of Cap Haitien. We left Yvon and called Delegue Ardrouin. It took a week or so but we finally got an appointment to meet with him. Again, after a very long wait, we were escorted into the Delegue's official office. We walked through curtains made of maroon velvet with tassels. It was air-conditioned and we were offered hot tea. This is not typical for offices in Haiti. There are 10 Delegues in the country of Haiti. They are much esteemed and have a lot of power. We told him of our legal situation, and he held up his hand and said, "Tann, tann" (wait, wait). He picked up his phone, and to our surprise, he called the First Lady of Haiti, Dame Sophia Martelly. She was President Martelly's wife. Unbeknownst to us the First Lady had already heard our plight. We're not sure who spoke with her but we are grateful. Delegue Ardrouin hung up the phone and said, "Dame Martelly told me to get your family back home." It was an order he'd received from the First Lady of Haiti. We could hardly speak. "Thank you, thank you, Delegue Ardrouin," we said. I hugged him before we left his office. It wasn't a week later and we were back in our homes at Kay Anj Village. We have Mayor Alteon, Delegue Ardouin, and Dame Sophia Martelly to thank for that. A few months later we were told the same family was continuing the unjust battle for our land. I reached out to Dame Sophia Martelly and Delegue Ardrouin again. Here is the actual letter I sent to them:

Good morning Dame Sophia Martelly and Delegue Ardrouin,

As you both know our dossier and case is in the Court du Cassasion (Supreme Court) currently. We have been told that we are safe in our Limonade village until the Court Du Cassasion makes a decision on our case.

Today we were told to go to Port Au Prince to meet with the DGI and Department of Justice. **We will go on Monday morning.**

The Pierre family who is illegally and unjustly trying to take our property (owned by the DGI) is active now as there is no current President.

Can you please help us? We believe in Haiti, the Haitian people, and we know that God has a plan. We also know there is a lot of injustice.

Dame Sophia, congratulations on all your wonderful work with the women of Haiti. You are an inspiration. I am deeply grateful for your help in the past with our situation.

Sincerely,
Debbie Harvey

A few months later, Delegue Ardrouin was promoted to Minister of the Interior for Haiti and would move to Port au Prince. This was good news for us as now we have a "friend" in the higher-governmental offices under the President in Port au Prince. On August 2, of 2016, I received a very unnerving phone call at my home in Virginia. It was Naomi telling me in a very strange-sounding voice, "There are some visitors here that must talk to you now." My heart began to race. *What now?* Naomi handed the phone to a man who introduced himself as Mr. Washington with the United States State Department from Port au Prince. My heart was now racing faster. Mr. Washington asked my name, my role at Kay Anj, how long I'd been working in Haiti, and many other questions. I had no idea why he was asking so many questions or for what reason he came from Port au Prince to Cap Haitien to come to our village. They then began asking questions about a former employee. Our Haitian manager, Mr. Charles, was employed by HHA for almost eight years. He was with us from the beginning. Mr. Washington asked what job Mr. Charles has at Kay Anj. How long did he work for us? What exactly did his role as Haitian manager entail? What was his role with our children and staff? I told them that Mr. Charles was no longer working for us. After almost eight years we began to see and witness behaviors that were not in line with our HHA mission. After a year or so of careful and thoughtful Board of Director discussions, we decided it was time to reduce Mr. Charles' responsibilities and his pay. He didn't like this at all. He was offended and very angry. He quit in March of 2016. Mr. Washington continued with the questions about Mr. Charles. When I told him that he quit his job in March he sounded very relieved. Naomi told me later that Mr. Washington moved off the front porch (where there were many people listening to his interrogation of me) of her house and into her bedroom where he could close the door for privacy. He then informed me that Mr. Charles, our former employee, had been convicted of a crime in the United States, and the State Department and the IBESR (Children's Services) needed to investigate him in Haiti. He told me they'd come to close our orphanage down.

Mr. Louis Mary, the Director of the IBESR in the North of Haiti, was a friend. We'd met him years ago and knew him as Piti Fwe. We first met while going through the expensive and time-consuming process to legalize our orphanage. He liked the way we ran our village. He told us he appreciated all we were doing for the kids in the North. It is because of our relationship with Piti Fwe that the United States State Department and the IBESR did not close us down. He told them of his relationship with us. That we were one of three legal orphanages in the North and in Haiti. He told them that we follow the rules and do all required to do in Haiti. He also told them that we truly love our children and our staff. We were told by Mr. Washington and the officials that drove in their three, blacked-out, black SUV's, that until the investigation is finished on Mr. Charles, our organization would be listed on the U.S. State Department watch list. You can imagine Mr. Charles was not happy. I arrived at our village a few days later and met with all of our staff. We put them all on three-month contracts (which they did not like at all) and told them they were prohibited from speaking with or having any contact with Mr. Charles. If they did they'd be fired on the spot. We told them we were on the watch list and we have to do everything they tell us to do and that they're telling us to have zero contact with Mr. Charles. Mr. Charles went to the high school

23 of our kids attend. He waited outside until they were finished with school for the day. He nicely spoke to them and reminded them that he was always good to them. He reminded them that he had not and would never do anything to harm them. The kids weren't sure what was happening so they continued to their bus for home. The next day we filed a restraining order with the Office for the Protection of Minors in Cap Haitien.

Mr. Charles was even more angry now. We have a nice, professional relationship with our local police officers so we asked them to drive by our village twice a week just so we would have police presence. This would send a message to Mr. Charles that he is not to come near our children or our village. While we sincerely believe Mr. Charles would not do anything to hurt us or our children, we do know that he spends his time with some unsavory characters. We must have our heads on a swivel, as Bill says. Always be aware of our surroundings and all those we're working with. A few months later, I wrote this letter to the United States Ambassadro to Haiti who I met at the Cap Haitien airport. We spent some time getting to know each other as I told him of our legal woes. He promised to visit our

Kay Anj Village and meet our wonderful family there. He never came. It reads:

> Good morning Mr. Ambassador and Mr. Hannan,
>
> You are aware that staff from your office recently visited our property in Dekle, outside Cap Haitien, on August 2 (Mr. Thompson and Mr. Robinson).
>
> Your staff and members of the Haitian IBESR informed us that a member of our staff, Mr. Charles, had a criminal conviction in the United States. This conviction took place in 1998. We were now aware of this conviction.
>
> We have terminated our relationship and informed our security guards that he will not be allowed back on our property. Since we received this information we have proactively taken steps to guarantee the safety of our children, including: We will hire a full-time security director from a professional security company in Haiti to train, monitor, and manage our security guards. We will pull background checks on all current Haitian staff and any future Haitian staff. And, before coming

with a group, we will pull background checks on all visitors and volunteers from abroad.

Do you have any other proactive suggestions for our operation here in Haiti and in the United States?

We have always had a respected, professional relationship with the local Government and Federal government in Haiti, and our United States Embassy. We will do whatever it takes to protect our children and continue our mission of educating them and helping them to grow up to one day help their country.

Respectfully,
Debbie Harvey

It's December 2016, and I am now staying at the Hotel Roi Christophe. Patrick, our new Chief of Security, and I agreed that I need to change up my routine. He said Mr. Charles is a criminal and is watching every move I make. He knows where I am throughout the day. I will have an armed, security guard beginning tomorrow until I leave. I told him that our Board of Directors emailed Mr. Charles and told him that we'd been advised by the U.S. State Department that we should not allow him on KAV property. He replied with, "Thank you." He smiled and said do not think for a second that he will lay low or be quiet. He said you think you know him but you don't. I've contacted my friend, Istvan Papp, at the United Nations, and asked that he have his men do a drive-by as well. They were not able to as there was no civil unrest at the time. He told me to call immediately if there was a manifestation or unrest of any kind. Istvan made sure I knew that "this is very serious." He is concerned for the perception of HHA and KAV. He informed us that our legalization is at risk, as Mr. Charles' name is on our land-lease documents. I cannot, strongly enough, recommend that you meet the people in positions of authority (both Haitian and American) while serving and working in Haiti. Today, Mayor of Cap Haitien, Yvon Alteon, who we met a couple years ago and is now a good friend, was promoted to Charge de Mission de la Region Nord (one of three in the country). He is personally helping us fight with the DGI and Domain in Port au Prince for our Kay Anj Village. He was instrumental in discovering that our DGI attorney, Mr. Toussaint, was dragging his feet and doing nothing for us. Bill and I, and our wonderful

Board of Directors, have complete faith that God's hand is all over this. We know it will be right in the end. We are protected and covered by the hand of God. It is written, "Greater is He that is in us than he who is in the world." We cannot be afraid. He continues to place people exactly where and when we need them to get through each tough situation we go through. For this we are grateful to Him.

Chapter 9:

LAFWA (DEEP FAITH)

> "God is our refuge and strength, an ever-present help in trouble. We will not fear, though the earth give way and the mountains fall into the sea." -Psalm 46:1-2

LET ME BEGIN WITH MY RELATIONSHIP WITH JESUS. I grew up Catholic. We didn't go to church every Sunday and our beautiful, white-and-gold bible sat on the living room table, the pages hardly ever touched. I didn't really know Jesus. My mom died 10 years ago and that's when I truly began my relationship with Jesus. I had nowhere else to turn after my mom's death. I began to pray. I met with our pastor, Pastor Barry, a few times and learned about how much better my life could be if I put Jesus at the helm. When we first began our organization the other members (good friends and a family member) of our newly-formed board thought we should be a secular organization "because we'd get more donations and grant money if we're not a Christian organization." I remember literally looking up at the sky and saying, "God, I can't believe this is what you want for us." It wasn't. How could it be? Bill and I told them we needed some time to think about it. We met with Pastor Barry who told us you can't fear what people think. You have to stand up for God. We knew it was God who founded HHA, not us. We told our board members that we would continue to follow and glorify God and remain a Christian organization. They all resigned on the same day.

Bill and I weren't sure where to go from there but we knew God would go before us and make the path clear. Boy, has He done that! I am often asked the question, "Why Haiti?" "Why don't you help people in the U.S.?" I struggled with how to answer this question for years. Today I am comfortable and confident in my reply. I pray and I listen, and then I go where God wants me to go. He asks many people to help the poor and impoverished in the U.S. I work in Haiti because I have received an invitation to do so by my God. He's asked me to join Him in His plans and purposes. Would it be much easier to serve in the U.S.? Absolutely! I am American and understand much of our culture here in the U.S. I am not Haitian and I am constantly learning about the Haitian culture and deep roots of the Haitian people. But God put me there and I believe He gives me exactly what I need when I need it to do what He wants me to do in Haiti.

Years ago I was having lunch with a wonderful, older (you'd never know she was 70!) woman who told me something I'll never forget. Joan and I were talking about my recent trials in Haiti. I was explaining to her that I felt deflated, done. I was frustrated, hurt, angry, and sad all at the same time. "Why would God have me go through all of this, Joan?" I asked her. I believe Joan has a red phone to Jesus. He speaks to her. It's her gift. Joan, with tears streaming down her face, looked at me intently, grabbed my hands from across the table and said, "Hold on, Jesus is telling me something." Every fiber of my body was hanging on her words. Joan closed her eyes, still tears streaming down her face, to listen to HIM. When she was sure she'd heard all from Him she looked at me squeezing my hands tightly and said, "God gave you a heart that beats for Haiti. He gave you this heart before you were ever born." Tears now streaming down my face (and I'm not a crier), I thanked Joan for the powerful message from God. I knew then that God would always give me whatever it was that He knew I needed for whatever trial or test He was putting me through at that time. I do not want to appear arrogant or self-important, but I do believe God has chosen Helping Haitian Angels. I believe He has chosen our organization to glorify and honor Him in Haiti. I don't think He has chosen any of us individually, but our HHA. He gives us small tests, and when we pray, listen, and obediently respond, I picture Him saying, "Thank you my good and faithful servants, here's another test, only it's going to be a bit tougher."

It was late 2013 and we'd spent the previous two years meeting with mayors, local-elected officials, attorneys, and notaries as we navigated the process of purchasing and leasing land in Haiti. We were meeting yet the third mayor of our local city to have him sign-off on all of our land documents. We stood in the middle of our property with blueprints spread across the hood of our truck. We pointed to our children's homes, school, church, medical/dental clinic, and sustainable farming. He asked if we would hire local men and women to work for us. "Absolutely," we said. He smiled and continued to study the blueprints. Why wasn't he asking any questions? He didn't say a word for what seemed like an hour. I'm sure it was just 10-minutes or so. He looked at me and our Haitian manager and said, as he was smiling from ear to ear, "Welcome home." The feeling was inexplicable. Elated, grateful, overjoyed, as we were on cloud nine! Finally, finally we can begin building. It was three, very long and arduous years to get here, but it was all worth it as we all shook hands and hugged over the blueprints on the hood of the truck. We were ready. Thank you God for your perfect timing. Our little, tiny church on our property has much meaning for all who come to Kay Anj village.

Before we built anything on our beautiful, loved land our board met over lunch to discuss our Phase 1 building. I sat very quietly as I listened to the men (I was the only woman) go back and forth about the children's homes and school. I sheepishly raised my hand and said, "Guys, I have something very important to tell you." They replied with, "Oh no, now what?" (And a little funny about how I am always changing things for them). I told them that I'd been fervently praying for our village, our kids, families, and through that prayer I felt the Lord telling me that we need to build our church first. Before our children's homes or school, our church needed to be built first. The guys hesitated for a moment, all looking at one another and said, "That's perfect, let's build the church first!" Our church opened its doors on Easter Sunday 2014. I saw this again as our Lafwa, or faithfulness to God. We only wish to glorify and honor Him.

We spoke in a previous chapter of our Kay Anj family's eviction at gunpoint in December of 2014. Minutes after they were removed from their homes we arrived at the place they would call home for just shy of three months. This is where true Lafwa filled every room, every person, morning, noon, and night. We found a box of moving blankets in the attic. We laid them on the tile floor and we had the biggest sleepover ever each night. Before going to bed, and again when they'd wake, and what seemed like all day, they all prayed together. They held hands and took turns praying. Then the little guys, all the way up to our mama's, recited Isaiah 41 over and over. Then they prayed individually. I've never seen such faith. Such deep Lafwa. They all believed and trusted God. They knew He would take care of them. They may have had peanut butter and jelly sandwiches every meal for a week but there was a peace in that house. A peace that surpasses all understanding. They knew He held them in the palm of His right hand. They trusted and had faith. Their faith could have moved every mountain in Haiti.

I told you about our attorney, Mr. Toussaint, in the previous chapter. There have been very few times in Haiti where I completely lost it. Even when I almost went to jail I kept it (pretty much) together. My nickname is Debbie Don't Play. I'm going to tell you about one of the exceptions. I'm not proud of it but it's real. Naomi (our incredible intern who lives at our village), Orano and I were in our attorney Charnel's office. We were calling Mr. Toussaint to find out if the third-strike document had been delivered to the family trying to take our land. Mr. Toussaint informed us that he needed to take a 30-day leave of absence from his job so that he could take care of his health. We were so close! *How could he now decide to stop the momentum? What was he trying to do? Did he have an ulterior motive?* Why, yes, he did. He told us that if we paid him (a lot of money) he would continue to work for us. I wanted to reach through the phone and grab him by the throat. I said, "I'm sorry, I must have misunderstood you Mr. Toussaint." He repeated exactly the same thing. I told Charnel that I wanted a new attorney. He advised me not to do that because no one else would want our case after Mr. Toussaint worked on it for two years (voodoo involved). I called my Bill and just cried. I had never been more angry, disappointed, and frustrated. I yelled and cried for 15 minutes on the phone to Bill and then to Charnel. It was so unfair and just wrong. How could he do this to us? I have a one-word answer: money. When I calmed down and we were headed down the long, narrow, wooden stairs to the outside, I apologized to both Naomi and Orano. I told them I am their leader and it was not right of me to lose my cool like I did. Naomi said, "It would have been odd if you hadn't lost it, Debbie." I hugged her and thanked her. Orano looked at me very seriously and said, "Let's go sit at the hotel, I need to talk to you." I felt like a child who'd just gotten in trouble. I knew he didn't appreciate my outburst and yelling. It was a short but very quiet drive to the hotel. Orano and I sat alone at a small table as the sun set above us. He looked at me, took a long, deep breath and said, "You cannot quit, Deb. God is using you to fight for your Kay Anj family. He needs you to fight for them. They do not have a voice, but you do. You cannot leave them. Please don't quit." I have never, in my life, felt the words of God spoken audibly through another human being that were so clearly meant for me. I grabbed Orano's hands and promised him I wouldn't quit. I made my Haitian family a promise long ago that I would never quit on them. So many had that came before me. Our kids who were abandoned, their parents quit on them. Our staff who had jobs with Americans before us. Those Americans quit on them and left when it got too hard or they couldn't find funding. They had all been quit on. I promised I would never join the group of people who quit on them. Never.

I am sure during that extraordinary conversation with Orano that the Holy Spirit spoke through him for me. I called Bill and cried once again. I felt a wonderful peace as Orano walked out of the hotel to find a tap tap home. I know that change is possible with the power of the Holy Spirit. I've witnessed it first-hand. That night in my room as I prayed alone on my knees on the cold, tile floor next to my bed, that I could relax in my faith, my Lafwa, trusting that God is able to do everything without my help. In fact, if we are God's children, then our problems are His problems. And He's much better at fighting our battles and solving our problems than we will ever be. Our job is to have deep Lafwa and trust Him to work everything out. Scripture says, "Don't be afraid," and "Don't be discouraged." When we face a seemingly impossible situation, we shouldn't be afraid and we shouldn't be discouraged. Has God ever lost a battle? No. God doesn't lose battles. Ever. Our faith teaches us to lean not unto our own understanding, but to trust in the God who created us and know that He will direct our path. As we all have experienced, that path isn't always as easy as we'd like it to be. This week at HHA in particular, we've been reminded of that. I spoke with Debbie yesterday, and she said, "It's been really hard to keep the faith, but without it we have NOTHING." She went on to say that despite the trials HHA has experienced in Haiti this week and this year, she has been encouraged by our kids and all of our staff coming together for fervent prayer. This week's tests, as Bill has mentioned, have even brought members of our community to their knees with us, joining us in prayer and singing songs of praises!

This is a letter our wonderful HHA staff member, Jessica, wrote when I couldn't be present at our 3rd Night of Hope Event. (Our Night of Hope Event is an evening where 50-plus couples get together for dinner to hear a Christian speaker, hear Debbie and Bill speak, and update on HHA and Kay Anj. It's not a fundraiser, just an evening to be with other Christian couples laughing, learning, and praying). The letter reads:

It goes without saying, Debbie really wanted to be at our Night of Hope tonight. There was an emergency at our village and she was asked to come immediately to take care of it. It would only be a couple days and she'd be right back to Virginia to help set-up for our 3rd Night of Hope. For weeks we have talked about how much the Night of Hope in April encouraged her and helped to renew her strength for the calling God gifted her in HHA. These are just two of many sources of encouragement this year. Our biggest source of encouragement however, continues to come from our 58 kids. As you know, we strive to provide a Christ-centered and loving home for them that they would have hope despite their abandonment, abuse, and orphaned status. We also pray they will be a catalyst for hope for their (and my) beloved Haiti. One of our Angels in particular, Debbie, wanted to talk about.

The first is our Daphnee, or Dafodil, as we affectionately call her. Dafodil has been with us from the very beginning in 2008. She had been physically and sexually abused and was impregnated by her father. She gave birth to a beautiful baby who was adopted and lives in the United States. To say she's had a tough time would be an understatement, and to be honest, we've had some tough times with her also. Earlier this year, she was kicked out of school for fighting after a classmate called her an offensive name. But last week, Daphnee was honored at her new school. She was chosen by her teachers and classmates for being such a great role model for the entire school. She is 1st in her English class and stays up each night, too, as Naomi, our American intern, to teach her new words. During our transitional-program ceremony, she told the entire board that she wants to be an ambassador—we all wanted to cry knowing her story.

During everything that's been going on, Daphnee has been the one to calm everyone down and say, "God is in control. Do not be afraid, this is just Satan because something great is happening here at Kay Anj—we must be tested!"

We are all called to serve. How we are called to do it may be different, but I have come to realize that service brings hope to people no matter what trial is before them and no matter what end of the service they are. Our faith continues to strengthen, and we are grateful to be people who can praise Him through any storm.

The last Wednesday of each month is HHA Prayer and Fast Day. Our prayer-team leader, Cathy Shaffer, allows God and the Holy Spirit to use her to bless all of us with the most powerful messages each month. We get together and pray in person, we thank God for all of His blessings, and we fast. The miracles that have happened on our prayer and fast days are simply incredible. From getting a call to meet at Starbucks to get an HHA update and then are handed a check to fund a medical clinic, to praying with mama's and kids for the loss of a wonderful Kay Anj family member. On one Prayer and Fast Day, Bill and I were visiting a friend in Ohio at a Skyline Chili restaurant. He'd been in Haiti with us for his first trip weeks before and was in the car when another organization handed us two brothers who'd been abandoned. Will, 7-years-old, wrapped his very thin arms around Jim's neck and wouldn't let go. Over chili, we told Jim how we needed to wait for electricity until transformers came in on a container. They had one now but it was super expensive. Jim got out a check and sponsored the boys for the year and paid for the expensive transformer. He said, "Take good care of those boys and go get your electricity now!" God continues to surprise us on prayer and fast days and all days. Trust in and rely confidently on the Lord with all your heart and do not rely on your own insight or understanding. "Trust in the LORD with all your heart and lean not on your own understanding; in all your ways submit to him, and he will make your paths straight." -Proverbs 3:5-6

Chapter 10:

CHILD REUNIFICATION AND FAMILY PRESERVATION

Deuteronomy 31:6 Be strong and courageous. Do not be afraid or terrified because of them, for the Lord your God goes with you; he will never leave you nor forsake you.

IN CHAPTER 2 WE TALKED ABOUT ORPHANAGES AND why we should not open a new one in Haiti. I also told you that I was embarrassed. Didn't I? If it didn't, I'm telling you now. I am well aware of Gods Perfect Timing. He is never early and He is never late. He is always right on time. His timing is Perfect. Our HHA is almost ten years old which is why this is difficult and causes me to feel a bit guilty. If God knew that

Orphanages were breaking up families, causing children to be abused and trafficked then why did He ask us to open one almost ten years ago? Let's refresh

An estimated 80% of children living in Haitian orphanages are not true orphans. Most of the children living in orphanages in Haiti have one living parent or relative who could possibly care for them. So, why the guilt I'm feeling? Did we separate or tear apart families? Did we remove children from loving mothers and fathers? We didn't know what we didn't know then and we are grateful for Gods continuing to stretch us and teach us what we now know.. Here's what we know now that we didn't know ten years ago (please understand that I don't feel the guild about this as I believe God has a plan for those He chooses. I believe He needed us to go through the trials and tests to get to the place where He has us today).

The primary reason that children end up in institutions is poverty and a lack of access to basic health, education and social services. Many parents of these precious children out of complete and utter desperation, place their children in orphanages hoping their children will receive better care than they believe they could provide. But, in many situations, this is not the case, as many orphanages cannot meet the basic needs of the children. Most donors support orphanages in Haiti with the best intentions to help the countries most vulnerable children. Yet, many children in Haitian orphanages have suffered violence, exploitation, abuse, and neglect. In the worst cases, orphanages were rampant with human rights abuses. Witnesses have described seeing physical (I've seen it myself) and sexual abuse, moderate to severe malnutrition and disease and severe neglect in many orphanages in Haiti. Young adults who had aged out of orphanages say they suffer from trauma, lack of education, unemployment and often homelessness. A few had networks of support or family ties. Many other children have been stolen, kidnapped or coerced from their families by black market baby brokers who sell them to orphanages who prefer to have them adopted internationally because it is more lucrative.

This discourages domestic adoptions in countries like Haiti. Often new adoptive parents have no way of verifying if the child they are adopting is in fact an orphan.

For all of these reasons, there is a resurgence of and renewed commitment to family preservation in Haiti and other developing countries. We at HHA agree and beginning in 2017 made a commitment to our children and their families to reunify those children in our Kay Anj family that it made sense to reunify. Our team in Haiti has and is working closely with IBESR (government department responsible for children) and have also been working with government and local partners to trace families and prepare these children and their families for reunification.

Family Preservation is defined as "the movement to help keep children at home with their families rather than in foster homes or institutions (orpahanges). This movement was a reaction to the earlier policy of family breakup, which pulled children out of unfit homes. Extreme poverty alone was seen as a justified reason to remove children." Family preservation advocates strive to protect children while empowering their families and communities. They believe that in most cases, children can best be protected by supporting their parents and/ or family member caring for the child. Family Preservation calls for extended family to be the first resource for children whose parents are not able or willing to care for them and for stranger placements to be a last resort. Please understand that Family Preservation does *not* advocate for allowing children to remain in abusive or severely neglectful homes nor forcing any mother who does not want her child to parent said child.

We, HHA, believe all children deserve homes and families –poverty should never be an acceptable reason for a child to be growing up in an orphanage. Although we provide exceptional, family home care in a safe and loving village, we view see our Kay Anj Village as the "best" last resort for orphaned and/ or abandoned children in crisis. We are not the authority for these children. The children are under the care of the IBESR, Haiti's Child Social Services. We do not "take in" children. Children are placed with us by Haitian Government agencies. With a position of humility we do our best to provide resources, plans, love and compassion to provide the country of Haiti the best family home care options for her most vulnerable children in crisis. We are providing an alternative to traditional institutional care for vulnerable orphaned and abandoned children by keeping helping families stay together. We are empowering caregivers and communities and serving as an advocate for transition to a family-first model with options for residential care when reunification is impossible. We provide holistic support and resources through our Family Preservation Program which allows families to keep or reclaim their children through microfinance, business training, adult education and school support. Of course there are situations when children should not be living with their biological families due to many different forms of abuse and other severe realities that threaten their safety. At HHA we provide family-style, residential care at our Kay Anj Village. These attachment-focused homes offer stability and a happy environment for children, surrounded by love and given the opportunity for a brighter future.

We believe that strong families are the most important source of material provision, spiritual guidance, and emotional support in the lives of children. Loving family members are crucial for child development – providing not the life sustaining food, water, clothing, and housing, but also a sense of identity and cultural understanding.

In Haiti there simply too many children growing up without their biological families. They grow up in and orphanage even though they may have a living parent or family member who they could live with. they have at least one living parent, and nearly all have extended families who could care for children with additional support. We need to remember that many of these parents simply cannot provide for their children. They may be homeless, have no job, be in abusive living situation. At HHA protecting children and preserving the rights of children are at the forefront of what we do. Loving parents and/or family members would be able to provide for their children if they had the support (education, food, clean water, clothes, skills training) to keep their children in the home with them. Children need consistent, loving adult care, which they can only truly receive from loving families. Orphanages, even those that are well run, cannot replace the love of a family. Crucially, children learn to make emotional attachments in families. And research proves that attachment is crucial to brain development and the development of cognitive and social skills. . We will continue to read reports on the Haitian orphanage crisis through the eyes of actual families we know and love. Many of our Kay Anj children are true orphans, that is not having a living mother or father. Some also have living biological relatives. Research strongly suggests that children do better and have more success in the future when they are raised in a home with their biological family. We now feel called and lead to reunify, when appropriate, some of our children with their biological relatives. This is a HUGE undertaking and means:

Ensuring there is a loving family member (preferably a mom or dad) to care for their child. We have learned that many children do not have a living mother or father so we will support a loving Grandparent, Aunt, Uncle etc.

We will continue to pay for education, books, uniform, meal at school, etc.

We will support the family with supplemental food monthly.

We will provide those who are interested, life and entrepreneurial skills training.

We will find jobs/microloan whenever possible for a member of the family. With 70% unemployment in Haiti this will be a difficult undertaking but we believe it is possible. We have been diligent about partnering wherever possible with other organizations. We have contacts that have employment opportunities for our family members.

We will conduct regular home visits to ensure our kids are loved, taken care of and academically supported. We plan to visit weekly after they are reunified. We will then go to twice monthly visits and then to monthly. We believe this new family preservation program will drastically multiply our impact in Haiti.

At HHA we plan to teach critical income-generating and entrepreneurial skills, and budgeting training. We employ only Haitians, enable children to attend our school, and support the economic development of families to empower parents to keep children where they belong – in their families and in their family homes.

As agents of change in Haiti, could we at the least agree to have conversations about the potential of reinvesting funding to support family and community-based interventions that are not only sustainable but preeminently better for children?

WE have the opportunity to improve the lives of hundreds of vulnerable children in Haiti. This requires understanding the needs of families and communities and respecting the rights of children.

As we said we work closely with IBESR. This year two of our children have been able to go home to their families with support and jobs for a family member. Nashcali had been with us for just under eight years. She was just about 7 years old when her mother fled to the Dominican Republic leaving her Aunt and grandma to care for her. Nashi was a strong willed child loving child. Aunt Jeanine had 5 children of her own and no real source of income. When she heard about the local pastor looking for children to put in an orphanage she reluctantly handed Nashi over. She would now spend the next 8 years at Kay Anj. Nashi was given nutritious food, clean water, a soft bed, a cutting edge education, the love of Jesus and a loving house mom. Nashi was truly loved. As Nashi got older we realized there were issues with her behavior. Clear signs of abandonment and attachment disorders. She made it difficult on her house mom and the other girls in her family style home. Nashi wet the bed every night (and sometimes during the day) and this continued as she became a teenager. Our on staff child psychologist talked with her regularly. Aunt Jeanine and Grandma visited each month. Nashi had never once said she was unhappy, wanted to go home. You see I have a theory. I believe the children who have a family member who visits regularly will never say that they want to leave and live with their family because the family will get very angry with them. The family has the best of both worlds. They know their daughter, grandchild, niece, cousin is in a loving home being given all the things the family cannot provide. And they get to visit. What could be better? So, the child never says a word but they begin to act out at around 12 – 14 years of age. My theory is that because they cannot say they want to go home to live with family, they act out so that we don't have a choice but to find the family and send them home. They know that we will continue to pay for their education so they will take the pain of an angry family for a short period of time (when sent home) over spending the next 5 years or so without their family. This is exactly what happened to Nashi. When we met with Aunt Jeanine she told us she could not take Nashi into her home. She talked about the expense, bet wetting, schooling etc. When we explained our reunification program, that we'd pay for school tuition, uniform, books, monthly rice and beans and also help Aunt Jeanine find a job, she agreed to work with us and give it a try. When Nashi saw her Aunt at Kay Anj she said "Debbie, am I going home?". I was sure she'd be devastated and so sad to leave us. I decided that Nashi was now 14 and could handle the truth. Yes, Nashi, you are going home to live with your Aunt Jeanine, Grandma and your cousins. She put both hands on top of her head and began jumping in circles. "when? When am I going home?" I was shocked at her response. I thought she'd say she didn't want to go but I was surprised to learn that all she wanted was to go home. I told her that we still had lots to work out as we wanted to make sure all was prepared for her. Aunt Jeanine needed to find the right school, get a uniform, find a mattress. Three days later Nashi, with her pillowcase full of clothes and sponsor letters, photos, toothbrush and notes from her Kay Anj family headed to her Aunt's home. She was quiet but excited. We visit Nashi every two weeks. She is doing so well in school that after Winter exams she was promoted to the next grade. Here's the best part...Nashi hardly ever wets her bed. She is comfortable with her family. She is happy at home.

Where reunification is not possible, where there is neglect and parental incapacity, more permanent, consistent and stable alternative care options may be pursued to support and provide for the child's safety and developmental, emotional and physical needs. One of the most difficult decisions for us in Haiti is deciding when and if it is in a child's best interests to be returned to their parents/family after the IBESR brings them to us for neglect or abandonment. Given our approach to practice that gives preference to family reunification, issues related to family reunification often do not improve with assistance. In some of these cases, parents have substance abuse or mental health problems which have not been assessed and which continue to endanger children. A percentage of parents have severe cognitive impairments as well as psychiatric problems. The children may have been chronically abused and/or neglected and experienced multiple forms of maltreatment, including emotional abuse or neglect.

Many parents just give up. The parents are living in a very difficult situation, they try to make do and take care of their children the best way they know how but they feel they don't have a choice and they walk away. In these cases we may be genuinely uncertain as to what it will take for these children to be be reasonably safe from further harm and or neglect. Often a mother or father remarries or has begun living with a new partner who may constitute a risk to a child he doesn't know. The mother may have a new baby, and the child being reunified could be put out on the street by the new husband/partner to bring in money or because he does not know or want anything to do with the child. We believe it is extremely dangerous to reunite a child with a parent who consistently experiences interactions with the child as painful, frustrating, irritating or infuriating, or as a sign of their own inadequacy. Most parents are likely to occasionally have negative feelings about their children, but also have a large reservoir of positive experiences that inhibit aggressive or distancing responses to children's difficult behavior. The measure of the success of treatment programs for neglecting parents who initially present as hopeless/helpless is not abstinence from drugs and alcohol, or the reduction of depressive symptoms, but the energy, initiative and hope to take on day to day challenges with a determined and persistent attitude.

An example of this is a family we call the Phodes. There is eldest brother Phodeles, sister Phodeline and youngest brother Ayisien. The Phodes lived at KAV for 6 months when their mom showed up one day to visit. We were told Mom had passed away. We talked with mom at length about her life, her love for her children and if it would be possible to reunify them with her. We watched to see if there was what appeared to be a bond between mother and children. We (and our Haitian staff) decided there was. The kids were thrilled to see her. Sat on her lap, she rubbed their backs and hugged them. We explained that we would help her find a job making blankets at an organization that supports moms with jobs so that they are not forced to put their children in orphanges. We told mom we'd pay for tuition and all related to school. We would provide monthly rice and beans for the family and she's have access to our counselor if needed. The kids went back home to live with their mom. A short five weeks later mom showed up at our gate with 7 year old Phodeline. Phodeline had (what a doctor said were) 2nd degree burns on both shoulders, armpit and face. After getting Phodeline taken care of by a doctor we sat with mom to try to understand what had happened and how she got burned. At first mom tried to blame Phodelines 5 year old cousin for playing with a plastic bottle that she got out of the fire. When we continued questioning her she finally broke down in tears. She told us that "she couldn't fully love her children because she couldn't take care of them the right way". I couldn't move. My heart broke for her and for her children. How could a mom not love her children? I don't believe she didn't love her children. I believe she couldn't allow herself to fully love them because she couldn't provide all that they needed. I believe the Phodes mother loved them. In fact, I believe she loved them very much. I will always believe that Phodeline got burned because mom knew the only way to get them back in the orphanage (and to stay in an orphanage) was to have something drastic happen to one of them that would prove to the IBESR that she was not capable of taking care of them.

In Haiti where there are few, if any, community resources available to support these impoverished families, parents need to be able to function independently before children are returned to their care and custody.

In order for a reunification to be successful we believe the parent child relationship must have interactions that create a nurturing intimate environment in which the child feel loved and protected. It is extremely dangerous to to reunite a legally dependent child with a parent who consistently experiences interactions with the child as painful, frustrating, irritating or infuriating, or as a sign of their own inadequacy. Most parents are likely to occasionally have negative feelings about their children, but also have a large reservoir of positive experiences that inhibit aggressive or distancing responses to children's difficult behavior. Absent periodic positive interactions between parents and children that strengthen affectionate bonds, power struggles within a family may easily escalate into physically and emotionally abusive behavior.

Research and those on the ground in Haiti confirm that reunification and family preservation can be achieved by creating sustainable, participatory, safe and evolving after care plans that strengthen the community's and the families' long-term capacity and by working one-on-one with parents and or other relatives. We will do this by Building strong partnerships with government departments and other peers. We will develope an Orphanage/Family Home Best

Practices to share. We will help find a job for at least one member of the family.

We will train and educate parents on life skills, vocational training, adult literacy, and assisting with micro loans. HHA has begun to accept children only through the IBESR, social services, and we try to be the last resort by helping struggling parents find resources they need so that they can keep their children at home with them and that alternative means of caring for a child should only be considered when, despite this assistance, a child's family is unavailable, unable or care for her/him.

HHA has begun to accept children only through the IBESR, social services, and we try to be the last resort by helping struggling parents find resources they need so that they can keep their children at home with them.

Chapter 11:

CONCLUSION

> "Give justice to the weak and the fatherless; maintain the right of the afflicted and the destitute. Rescue the weak and the needy; deliver them from the hand of the wicked."
> -Psalm 82:3-4

THE TRIALS AND THE TESTS ARE REAL. YOU HEAR OVER and over Haiti is hard. Haiti IS hard. There is corruption, cultural misunderstanding, preconceived ideas, and spiritual warfare. This is Haiti. Haiti will make you much closer to Jesus, or it will make you go home. The enemy's goal for all of us serving in Haiti is to make it so difficult, heartbreaking, and frustrating that we want to hop on the next American Airline's flight and head home. The enemy will make it so hard that we never want to return. Haitians, because their faith has been crafted through hardships and daily-life struggles, have faith that puts ours in the United States to shame. Allow their faith to challenge and strengthen you. Allow them to encourage and strengthen you. Live humbly, and get down on their level. Live WITH them as family would. Hold their babies, eat with them, go to the market with them, talk late into the night with your staff or those you live with, pray on your knees with them, cry with them, and laugh with them. When we build deep and honest relationships, not based on money, we begin to give respect and earn respect, then and only then are we both able to trust. Tell them you appreciate them, you value their insight, and you would like their advice. I once had a Haitian tell me they'd never had an American ask their advice. They're Haitian, we are not.

Serving and loving in Haiti is one of the most difficult and yet special things I've ever done. There is a very steep, learning curve that most of the time we are not able to fully understand. We will never and should never feel like we have it all figured out. We enter a country with a deeply-rooted culture, complex history, and insanely difficult challenges just to survive day to day. We have created some of these problems for them. I'm not for a second saying that we should all leave Haiti, though there are some who say we should. If God is calling you to Haiti, and it truly is your calling, you will need to press into Jesus more than you ever have. A friend of mine once told me that it's much easier to see, feel, and hear Jesus on a dark backdrop. If you don't live in Haiti, but you travel there often, know that finding the balance between your family you've left in the United States (or any other country) and your family in Haiti is very difficult. Bill and I went through years of struggles trying to figure out where God wanted us, our marriage, our kids in Virginia, and our family in Haiti. Always remember it's tough, but you are there for THEM and not for you. Be prepared for betrayal, heartbreak, frustration, discouragement, feeling used, lies, and deception. You will experience every one of these if you're serving in Haiti. It's part of the deal when you agreed to go. We should have run from Haiti more times than I can count on two hands. But, when we learn how to humbly love, work with, and how to wage war against the spiritual realm, then the country of Haiti becomes a magnificently beautiful place to lay down our lives. We will always walk humbly living Christ-like, loving, and honestly. We will continue to fail-forward.

Are you struggling in Haiti? Not sure how to hire an attorney, or if you even need one? Not sure if your mission groups and volunteers are truly helping and not hurting? Are you wrestling with where to turn next? Fighting spiritual warfare? I keep an updated list of documents and resources in a toolkit for you at www. AngelsAdvisoryGroup.com. So keep that web page bookmarked and come back regularly, as I am continually researching and adding to the list.

THANK YOU

I'VE WANTED TO WRITE THIS BOOK FOR YEARS. GOD had a bigger plan. He continued to test me and our Helping Haitian Angels organization. He knew I needed more chapters in this book. He wanted me to learn more so that I could fail-forward and pass on the information he was blessing me with so that others just beginning the process, or struggling through the process, could benefit from all He put us through. He wanted to see how we would respond. Did we do what we wanted to do when tested (the easy route), or do we respond by stepping out in faith while undeniably trusting Him? Do we glorify Him in each decision we make? In 2008, I made my first trip to Haiti. I had no desire to ever go to Haiti. Today we have 58 of the most amazing, loving, funny, goofy, bright kids who all have stories of their early lives that we can't even comprehend. They have all been abandoned, orphaned, and been unwanted. Some have had parents who tried to kill them. These are my children. They are my loves. The adults who work with us are just as special as the children. They are Jesus-loving, role models who dance, sing, help with homework, protect us, and respect all we're doing for them. They are also my family and I adore each and every one of them. Thank you God for this gift. The gift of a big, huge, Haitian family.

To all of our volunteers, I am humbled by the hours they spend loving our children and building relationships with them. You sweat, cry, hurt, get frustrated, and they LOVE. You get your hearts dirty, not your hands dirty. You build people and not buildings. And you listen to all my crazy stories! I am grateful for your sacrifice. You sacrifice time away from family and work, you sacrifice financially, and you sacrifice emotionally. Haiti is hard.

We would not be able to feed or educate one child if it wasn't for our generous donors. We thank you for your belief in us and all God has us doing in Haiti. We thank you for your trust that we are using your gifts wisely and carefully. You sponsor our children which makes them the happiest children on the planet. They pray for you and wait for you to come visit. You give them hope. You let them know that they matter. Thanks to you they believe they can go on to university and become a doctor, teacher, a business person, and a good mom and/or dad.

I've told my board and others who will listen that we have the best board in the whole, wide world. You listen, guide, advise, and are without question the most supportive and faithful group of friends I've had the pleasure to work with. Each one of you plays a very special role at Kay Anj. God brought us all together for an amazing family.

Without Cathy Shaffer and her prayer team we would be lost. They pray and fast monthly, have emergency-prayer meetings (when we're in trouble in Haiti!), and pray for our children and volunteers by name. They have the direct line to God and we are grateful.

They call it my "God job." Will, Jake, and Becca, my three, wonderful children, have supported me and encouraged me to ride this crazy, Haiti, roller coaster since I returned from my first trip in tears. They have each been with Bill and I in Haiti too many times to count. They love and adore their Haitian brothers and sisters. I know there were times I put Haiti and our family there ahead of them. They knew it, too. I'm sure it hurt, but they loved me and supported me through it. It was definitely hard at times, finding the balance, but again, Will, Jake, and Becca gave me grace and encouraged me to focus on Haiti.

ABOUT THE AUTHOR

IN 1986, DEBBIE MARRIED OHIO STATE BUCKEYE FOOTball player, William (Bill) Harvey, and moved to Northern Virginia. As a wife and mother of three young children, and after many invitations by her husband to visit one of the poorest nations in the world, Debbie reluctantly agreed to a short trip to Haiti. This was the trip that changed her life.

Debbie left Haiti with a shocking glimpse into the starvation and homelessness of Haitian children and made an agreement with her husband to give her emotional struggle of wanting to help these children 30 days. Bill believed that in 30 days, these feelings would fade and their lives would return to normal. This is where Debbie's heart was transformed and the **"Helping Haitian Angels"** story begins, and her successes and failing-forward experiences now help thousands of people to take the leap of faith that she blindly accepted. Debbie believes that her heart for Haiti is not something that she developed, but instead, a divine calling and gift. When looking back at the struggles, tests, and lessons-learned, she believes that not knowing where each day, month, and year would lead, has been her biggest blessing.

While building Kay Anj Village, a non-profit (501c3) organization, Helping Haitian Angels, which includes an orphanage, school, dental facility, transitional homes, volunteering housing, and self-sustaining gardens built on over 40-acres of country land, Debbie researched for answers to common questions that would have saved their organization hundred-thousands of dollars, time, and heartbreak. Every path to Debbie's inquires led to dead-end roads. Through her tears, frustration, fears for her life, and freedom, and a passion to help other organizations develop. Now Debbie offers her journey as an insightful, humorous, and heart-warming story of how to do things the right way. Most organizations begin with genuine intentions to help the poor in Haiti, but unintentionally fail to understand that helping can also hurt, if not done correctly. Debbie now uses her fail-forward message to lead other organizations to success and to avoid costly and damaging mistakes. The **Angel Advisory Group (AAG)** offers a straightforward path that leads organizations to a successful journey forward. More information can be found at www.angeladvisorygroup.com.

Debbie and Angeline embracing as Angeline is reunified with her mother, brother and sisters.

Debbie and then President of Haiti, Michel Martelly.

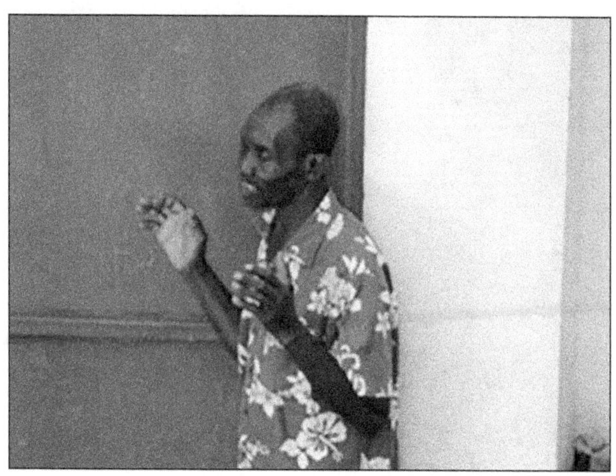

Clauvis (our Kay Anj security guard) who has since passed away, would pray for every child in Kay Anj, by name, every day.

UDMO Police, Haitian Police - 18 men with AR-15's evict our Kay Anj family at gunpoint.

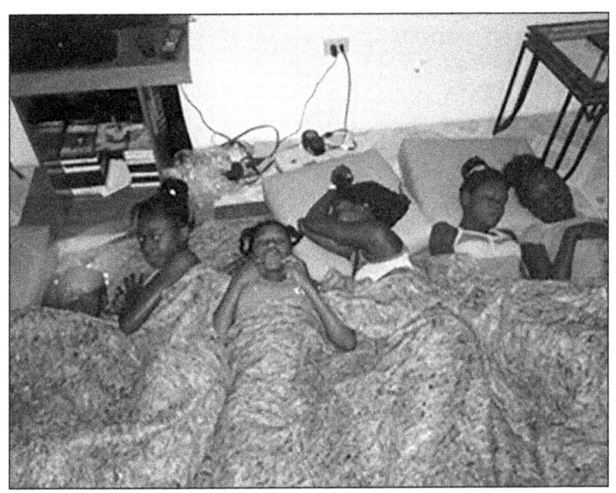

Our girls trying to sleep the night we were evicted. All kids and mama's lived in a 2 bedroom house for 10 weeks

The family (Hilaire) who illegally tried to take our property spray painted their name on our gate.

Bill and Debbie Harvey in Haiti.

Our Manmi Rose on the stand as a witness
for Debbie in the Appellate court.

Debbie fighting to stay out of jail in the Appellate
court of Cap Haitien.

CPSIA information can be obtained
at www.ICGtesting.com
Printed in the USA
BVHW040928030219
539333BV00027B/814/P